SOUTH OF THE HIMALAYAS

One Hundred Years of Methodism in India and Pakistan

by
JAMES K. MATHEWS

Executive Secretary, Division of World Missions
Board of Missions of The Methodist Church

Introduction by
E. STANLEY JONES

Editorial Department
JOINT SECTION OF EDUCATION AND CULTIVATION
BOARD OF MISSIONS OF THE METHODIST CHURCH

Printed in the United States of America
at
The Parthenon Press
Nashville, Tennessee

FIRST EDITION

TO

Eunice and countless others who have helped me to understand and to love the people of India and Pakistan.

TABLE OF CONTENTS

INTRODUCTION

It is not easy to interpret modern India. It is so complex and so changing. Visitors to India for short periods may fasten on interesting facets of India's life and lose sight of the total picture. They may be very misleading. On the other hand, missionaries, who are engrossed in a local task and a local situation, may fail to see the whole even though they have spent decades in India. Really to interpret India and the church there a man must be especially qualified.

The writer of this little book is especially qualified to interpret India. He has served years in India as a missionary and as an army officer. When he left the army, he became secretary for India with the Methodist Board. From that position he could see the total picture in its total context. While secretary he has made a number of visits traveling the length and breadth of India and Pakistan, studying problems and possibilities at first hand.

Now that Dr. Mathews has become Executive Secretary of the Division of World Missions, in addition to retaining the secretaryship for India, he sees India in an even wider context of the total missionary movement.

Perhaps the thing that has given him the most penetrating insight into this new India is his intensive study of the life and teaching of Mahatma Gandhi. He has chosen the Father of the New India—Gandhi—for his research for the Ph.D. degree at Columbia University. He has gone into the whole range of literature in East and West on Gandhi and has seen him from all angles in the context of the struggle for independence—and afterwards.

But more than perhaps anything else, the writer has the insight that comes from a sympathetic attitude toward India. When one lacks that insight, the meaning of this new India does not open. India becomes a bundle of problems. But with sympathetic insight India is no longer a problem, she is an infinite possibility. Problems there are—plenty of them, but possibilities there are—an amazing amount of them. Dr. Mathews glances at these problems and gazes at these possibilities. He leaves the reader with a warm sense of opening vistas and bristling possibilities. India is seen here in relation to its neighbor, Pakistan. It must also be thought of in relation to its larger neighbor, China.

For India and China are the focus of the world's attention—China undertaking to make vast changes under Communism and compulsion; India undertaking these changes under freedom and democracy. The one that produces the better order may determine the future of the whole of the non-Communist East. So India is important—very.

Dr. Mathews believes in this new India and in the role of the church there. On her independence, he urged the mission boards to show their faith in this New India by giving of their best. Now that we are going through a period of strain in regard to Christian missions, he still believes in India and would urge us again to give India our best—especially our understanding sympathy.

Seldom has a writer brought to his task of interpretation more qualifications than the author of this book. This is an important book about Southern Asia and the hundred years of work there by the Methodist Church, set amid the work of other Christian denominations.

E. STANLEY JONES

CHAPTER I

A LOOK AT THE CHURCH IN SOUTHERN ASIA

SEVERAL YEARS ago some Methodist missionaries were accompanying Mahatma Gandhi on his morning walk. He often combined such conferences with his exercise. He said to them: "So you are Methodists! John Wesley would hardly recognize you today, would he!" Was Gandhi right? This little volume describing one hundred years of Methodist activity in Southern Asia may suggest an answer.

The Wider Setting

Of course, Methodism cannot be isolated from the total Christian witness in that vast area. Altogether there are approximately ten million Christians, about equally divided between Catholics and Protestants, in these two countries. This total number is exceeded in Asia only in the Philippines. India numbers more Protestants than any other country of Asia.

Though Christians make up but a little more than two per cent of the population, their influence is far out of proportion to their numbers. It has been said that about one eighth of the organized medical work in India is under Christian auspices. In the two countries today there are under Protestant care approximately 277 hospitals with about 18,000 beds; 278 dispensaries; 12 tuberculosis sanatoria; 70 leprosy hospitals with 8,500 in-patients; 75 nurses' training centers, including one for public health nurses; 15 training schools for midwives; 10 for laboratory technicians; 2 medical schools; one school for radiologists; one psychiatric clinic. Turning to education, Protestants operate 45 colleges; 448 high schools; 553 middle schools; about 15,000 primary schools; 109 teachers' training schools; 36 theological institutions; 71 Bible schools. To this may be added special schools for agriculture, industrial work, social work, and orphanages. There are approximately 25,000 organized or unorganized congregations. There are 42 Protestant printing presses. What Methodists are doing must always be thought of as just a part of this larger whole.

A further qualification is necessary. It is not proper to speak of Methodism in India solely with reference to missionary efforts stemming from American Methodism. Very important work has been done in Southern Asia by British Methodists as well. Indeed, it will be recalled that Thomas Coke, following his stay in America, died in 1814 aboard a vessel sailing from Britain to establish work in Ceylon. The effort there was begun by his colleagues and later spread to the Indian peninsula. The majority of Methodists of this background have since 1947 been related by union to the Church of South India.

Indirect Influence

If Methodists share in the visible aspects of the whole church in Southern Asia, they share also in the indirect contribution Christianity has made there. In some respects this indirect influence is more impressive than the direct. There are undoubtedly many Indians who are private or secret Christians, not having accepted the sacrament of baptism and membership in a church. It is also evident that Christianity has leavened many aspects of life in both of these countries. Countless Indian lives have felt the touch of Jesus Christ, and not in vain.

It is perhaps better for non-Christians to evaluate these intangible results of Christian activity. This they frequently do. It is not uncommon for a Hindu to admit: (1) that Christianity has stimulated reform within Hinduism, so that it has been cleansed of some of the unhappy practices it once sanctioned; (2) that Christian standards of morality are widely accepted in India, though as in the West, often honored by the breach; (3) that the church has performed much service of obvious good to society, particularly in education and medicine; (4) that Christianity has supported progressive measures in Indian life; (5) that Christian missionaries and their Indian colleagues have pioneered in all manner of undertakings which have resulted in uplift for India.

It is of interest, tinged perhaps with irony from the British point of view, that those who most actively led the Indian national movement were precisely those most exposed to Western and Christian influences.

Sometimes acknowledgment of all this is almost unconscious. Non-Christians may say: "We must show a missionary spirit." A Hindu professor to Sikh and Muslim students who were arguing suggested: "Why don't you solve your quarrel in a Christian way?" At one time every Indian Cabinet member had a Christian confidential secretary.

At other times acknowledgment is more specific. A Muslim Minister of Education in one of the states in explanation of new progressive measures in his department stated: "You must not forget that I spent four years in a Christian high school." A Hindu college president: "The greatest thing that Christian missions have done is to give back to the outcastes the humanity we took from them." A well-known leader of a Hindu sect to an Indian Methodist preacher: "You Christians know how to serve; we Hindus can never seem to do the way you can." A Muslim: "Christians are the only ones who have done any real social work." A letter from a non-Christian, writing appreciatively to a mission school principal, closed with: "My daughter wants to be a journalist. Please put her name on your list. She will be a month old next week." A Brahmin governor of Assam, perhaps in a moment of enthusiasm, said: "The one jet of light in these hills of Assam is the work of Christian missions. Take it away and all is darkness." Finally, a great Hindu reformer, Sir Narayan Chandavarkar, once stated: "The ideas that lie at the heart of the gospel of Christ have been slowly, but surely, permeating every part of Hindu society and modifying every phase of Hindu thought." [1]

Gandhiji himself often paid tribute to Christ, though he frequently with considerable justification was a friendly critic of Christian missions. He said in a speech at Delhi to the Inter-Asian Relations Conference in 1947 that the future of the world must be based on two things: (1) searching for truth to make us free, and (2) establishing international relations on love.

Upon the death of Gandhi observers were not slow to point out that he, like Jesus, was killed on Friday; that he was slain due to the treachery of one of his fellow Hindus; that as Jesus was wounded in the hands and feet and side, so Gandhiji was pierced by three assassin's bullets. Newspaper accounts constantly used Christian terms to describe him. Quite evidently he had "outgrown" similarity to the many Hindu deities. On the Sunday following his death Mrs. Sarojini Naidu, the silver-tongued orator and poetess, in a radio speech cried: "O Gandhiji, come back to us! This is Sunday, Resurrection morning!"

Without doubt the indirect deposit has been very great. This subject is, however, one to be viewed by Christians with restraint, humility, and frank recognition of many shortcomings and failures.

"A Cloud of Witnesses"

The official title of the church related to American Methodism is the Methodist Church in Southern Asia. It is sometimes called "Mecosa" for short, the cable address of our church in Bombay. Like the blind men touching an elephant and likening it in turn to a wall, a snake, a rope, a tree, so Mecosa means many things. This reference is, by the way, not out of place;

---

[1] Quoted in *India and the Passing of Empire,* Sir George Dunbar, Nicholson and Watson, London, 1951, p. 5.

for the story of the blind men and the elephant originated in India.

Mecosa means people. The Methodist Church in Southern Asia has a membership in all categories totaling 554,000. Of these a little more than 35,000 are in Pakistan. It should be borne in mind that there are about as many Methodists in these lands as in all the more than forty other countries in which effort overseas is carried on by the Board of Missions of The Methodist Church.

Mecosa suggests tremendous variety and geographical range. Methodist churches are organized in three of Pakistan's five provinces and fourteen of India's thirty states. Probably few, if any, people could follow Methodist worship in all of its churches in the subcontinent, for it is carried on in eleven different languages and a number of related dialects. No one person has ever seen all the Methodist work, for it extends from scores of centers into several thousand villages. A recent visitor reported that in his travels to see Indian Methodism he had utilized planes, trains, a boat, cars (including a jeep), a motorcycle, bicycles, two types of carts drawn by bullocks or oxen, three kinds of horse-drawn vehicles, three kinds of rickshaws, the backs of a horse, camel, and elephant—and had walked!

Nor does even this give an adequate picture. It is not very well known that Methodist work in Burma, Malaya, and the Philippines was started from India. Thus at one time "Indian Methodism" spanned the five thousand miles from Karachi to Manila!

Mecosa means Christian service through institutions. It is hard to make statistics live, but they do help us to comprehend something of a complex range of activity. The Methodist Church of Southern Asia is organized into four episcopal areas, ten annual conferences, and 64 districts. There are approximately 300 organized churches and more than a thousand preaching points. A total of 1,962 Sunday schools are reported and 123 youth societies. There are 487 women's societies.

Turning to education, in these conferences there are 516 village primary schools with more than 11,000 pupils. Of other schools there are 121 at primary, middle, and high school levels attended by more than 30,000 students. The two Methodist colleges in Lucknow, Isabella Thoburn and Lucknow Christian, accommodate about 400 and 800 students respectively.

For the ministry of healing there are 14 hospitals of various sizes and 27 dispensaries touching the lives of thousands of people each year.

This is not to mention at this point the other types of activity—social work, care of orphans, efforts in behalf of temperance, relief work of various types, and a host of other functions being carried on by our church or in co-operation with other denominations. Indeed it might be said that no activity associated with the church in the West is entirely lacking in these mission lands. The missionary effort is in a real sense the projection overseas of the whole life of the church. Furthermore, new types of work are constantly being devised to meet situations peculiar to a given area and time.

Mecosa means Methodists who serve. At the time of writing—the spring of 1955—there are 325 Methodist missionaries assigned to India and 33 to Pakistan. Of these missionaries 151 are serving under the Woman's Division of Christian Service and 207 are related to the Division of World Missions. They are greatly outnumbered by the approximately 1,300 women and 2,200 men of these two countries who serve in the comradeship of the gospel in many types of service—as teachers, nurses, doctors, preachers, evangelists, administrators, to mention only some of the categories. Methodism actually and potentially is a tremendous force for good in Southern Asia.

The Spirit of Jesus

Of more importance than numbers and types of undertaking is the question of whether or not something of the Spirit of Jesus Christ is being reproduced in the lives of people. Our tendency is either to underestimate or overidealize in replying to such questions about so-called "mission lands," but the answer is undoubtedly in the affirmative. Upon the lives of countless Christian Indians is found the stamp of Christ with unmistakable genuineness. Let us meet a few of them.

Mrs. Deborah Luke, the widow of the Rev. Benjamin Luke, lives at Sironcha in the heart of India. She is known as Lukamma—Mother Luke. Now over eighty, which is very old for India, Lukamma possesses a timeless beauty of one who has for years walked with God and seemingly never missed a step.

Brought as an orphan at the age of six to a girls' school in South India, she has lived her life in Methodist surroundings. In her late teens she married Benjamin, a convert from caste Hinduism. He was to have been the headman of his village near Bangalore, but as punishment for becoming a Christian he lost his inheritance, had his tongue branded, and was for twenty-four hours suspended by his hands. In 1899 they were assigned by Bishop Thoburn to the jungle station of Sironcha. There he was a powerful preacher and an able superintendent until his death in the influenza epidemic of 1918.

After his death Lukamma on examining his postal savings book found the credit amounted to the equivalent of a few cents. She was also struck by the marked passages of his Telugu Bible stressing that the Lord himself was the "inheritance" of those left without material legacy. Since then she has lived a life of faith. She says: "My children do not need to care for me. God's Son does." Her motto is Psalm 37:25: "I have been young, and now I am old; yet have I not seen the righteous forsaken, nor his seed begging bread."

Lukamma lives a sustained and devoted life of prayer. It is not mere sentimentality but a fact to report that two spots on the carpet beside her bed are worn thin through her habitually kneeling there in prayer. Her influence on Christian and non-

Christian alike is wide and profound, for the touch of saintliness deeply impresses India.

From her Christian home came four children. A son is now
a district superintendent and an evangelist effective in four
different languages. One daughter is an educator, principal of
a Methodist school. She reported recently: "All the students
in my school (nearly 400 of them) are Christians except thirty.
We are working on the thirty." Two daughters are doctors, one
in Government service and one in the little Methodist hospital
at Sironcha.

From this one Christian home came an evangelist, an agent
for winning hundreds into the kingdom; a teacher who has
helped to bring a more abundant life to hundreds of children;
and two doctors who have caused thousands to feel the healing touch of Jesus Christ. This is a tribute to the character
of Mother Luke. In her we see the simple faith of a devoted
Christian Indian at its best.

Incidentally, years ago a Methodist layman on Long Island
gave a special gift for several years to help support the work
of Benjamin Luke. Doubtless he did not realize fully what it
did. Surely in the economy of the kingdom that investment
will pay dividends eternally.

Or meet Shankarappa. He is a leading layman of a village
in the South India Conference. He is outstanding as an example of what can take place in the life of a person of unpromising outcaste origin. His character evidences a considerable measure of natural ability transformed by the grace of
Christ.

In 1910 he was baptized, and for him this step meant a
serious withdrawal from his earlier non-Christian practices. He
immediately set about the amendment of his own life and active witness to others. Within his village orbit he has demonstrated a passion for social righteousness. He has given liber-
ally of his means that others might hear the gospel.

The witness of Shankarappa often takes forms utterly alien

to our culture but intensely relevant to his own. For example, he defies many local superstitions. In his locality a manger is always constructed with the ends extending east and west. His manger runs north and south. Tradition says it is unlucky to have an even number of sections between the beams of the roof. Shankarappa built an even number. Tradition also dictates that a pillar should not be in front of the door. His house has one there. Some of his neighbors consult an astrologer about the date for sowing seed. He deliberately plants at another time. Then, because he uses more enlightened methods of cultivation, his crops are the best in the village. Trivial matters? About them is a holy boldness because of which his neighbors are shedding some of their shackles. Many of them have followed him into the liberty of Jesus Christ.

Shankarappa is the most trusted man in his village. People of every Hindu caste seek his judgment on their problems. Age and infirmity are overtaking him but his eye is clear; his witness is strong. His life reflects the mastery of the Spirit of Christ.

Or meet a nameless policeman. A new missionary saw him on a railway station platform. It was the missionary's first rail journey upcountry. After a cramped night on the train he descended at a station and walked up and down the platform. A policeman tried to speak to him, but he did not know the policeman's language nor the policeman the missionary's. Suddenly the policeman began to whistle. The missionary recognized the tune and whistled the second stanza with him. It was "What a Friend We Have in Jesus!"

They thought they had no common language, yet they discovered that after all they did. It was the universal language of Christian love. They were two individuals who had responded to the friendship of Jesus. Hence, they were friends. They never met again, but in that moment it was clear that something of the Spirit of Jesus had been communicated to that Christian Indian, prompting his unique confession of faith.

Bringing the Picture into Focus

We have mentioned the tendency both to underestimate and to overidealize the church. This is true when we think of the church during the first century. It is true when we think of such lands as India and Pakistan. Methodism, at any rate, *is* in its first century in these countries. There is, therefore, more similarity between its congregations and the church at Corinth than there is between one of them and a church in, say, Kokomo, Indiana! A little New Testament realism will help us to observe spiritual vitality amidst many depressing and disheartening conditions.

The number of Christian Indians and Pakistanis is not only proportionately small; they are also, for the most part, of very lowly origin. Not fewer than 80 per cent originated from the outcaste group. This is nothing to be ashamed of; they came to Christ because of their abysmal need. Fortunately some depressed-class people don't know they are depressed.

A high-caste Hindu was asserting that there were sufficient resources in Hinduism for India's spiritual needs. He was asked: "But what of the untouchables?" To which he replied: "Oh, only a Christ can lift them." In some instances these people have not moved very far from their former manner of life. This process takes time. Some who are already Christian express regret when more folk of this origin enter the church, for their presence at first lowers the average level of Christian attainment and thereby adversely affects the prestige of the community. Nevertheless, a steady stream of these unlikely people make their way to the cities and help to form strong congregations there.

Moreover, the average Christian is desperately poor. The per capita income for India is about $55 per year; probably less in Pakistan. Even this wealth is not evenly distributed. A wage of about ten cents a day for some kinds of work is not uncommon. In some instances day laborers receive more than a village pastor. This poverty is one reason why the church has not become more fully self-supporting. This is one of the acute problems of Methodism in Southern Asia, but progress is being made.

If the average Christian is poor, so also is his non-Christian neighbor. It should be no comfort to us that many of them have never known more abundance and so perhaps have greater resources for endurance of hardship than we. Hunger for them is experienced in the same part of the anatomy as with us. To see deprivation of one's children involves for them the same kind of parental heartache as for us.

Many Pakistani and Indian Christians are illiterate. The literacy rate within the church is not more than 30 per cent. This is high when compared with the nationwide average for India of about 20 per cent and for Pakistan of about 10 per cent. Several factors are important to keep in mind. First of all, illiteracy is by no means the same as ignorance. Many a person who cannot read gives evidence of immense practical knowledge and intelligence. Furthermore, we need to recall the low literacy rates even today in some Western countries, such as Italy with almost 70 per cent illiteracy, Spain and Portugal with about 50 per cent. As late as 1900 in the United States 25 people out of every 100 could not read and write. Nevertheless, there are no grounds for complacency while any child of God is deprived of immediate and personal access to God's Word.

The church is largely rural. This is not surprising in countries where nine out of ten live in villages. It should be recorded, however, that Christians tend to gravitate toward the city, for 20 per cent of them are urban dwellers as opposed to 10 per cent for the general population of India. Ofttimes the village Christians are scattered with only a few families in each of dozens of communities. This is particularly the case in North India. This works against a feeling of Christian solidarity and makes adequate pastoral care extremely difficult. It is not uncommon for a pastor to be assigned to a score of villages. An outstanding case is that of a pastor in North India who with two helpers is responsible for 10,000 Christians in 180 villages! It is also difficult to persuade the city-trained teacher or preacher to serve in distant and drab rural surroundings. Nevertheless they do go, often with deep dedication. As one remarked: "If I did not have the love of Christ in my life and a burning passion for him, I would have left this village in ten days!"

It may be observed that very often Christians are docile and seemingly lacking in dynamic, yet bickering and lawsuits within the church are all too frequently encountered. Someone has said that not one in five is a convinced and committed Christian. We may ask ourselves whether or not the record is any better in the "Christian" West. Some have indeed "lost their first love." There is evidence of self-centeredness among folk who have for years been impressed with the necessity of "*self*-support, *self*-government, *self*-propagation" of the gospel, yet there is often overdependence on foreign resources.

If these shortcomings were the whole picture, it would be sad indeed. But some of the seeming limitations of the church are not limitations at all. Poverty, lowly origin, humble surroundings may be marks of kinship with Jesus. This is a "day of small things." We have learned to know the potency of the microscopic—the atomic. Paul's words immediately occur to one: "God chose the foolish things of the world, that he might put to shame them that are wise; . . . the weak things of the world, that he might put to shame the things that are strong; . . . the base things . . . the things that are despised . . .: that no flesh should glory before God" (I Cor. 1 :27-29; A.S.V.).

There are many commendable aspects of the church. It often displays an amazing vitality. This strength is indicated by the steadfastness of so many Christians at a time when it is no longer profitable to be a Christian, if it ever was profitable—even during British rule. It is seen in the endurance of those who not infrequently experience in certain localities discrimination and some form of persecution for their faith, yet have taken gladly the "spoiling of their goods." It is demonstrated by the number of villagers who voluntarily give their Christian witness to their neighbors.

In many sections the church is showing missionary zeal. This is true at the Christian conventions or spiritual life conferences in so many places in West Pakistan. There are many signs of the ancient church of Travancore increasingly breaking its silence and giving throughout the subcontinent the type of leadership it should give as the most sophisticated and oldest Christian tradition in the country. During early 1954 a choir of Christian hill-tribesmen from Assam toured India singing and witnessing with remarkable effectiveness. Two generations ago their ancestors were head-hunters.

The church has a surprising pool of able leaders, though never enough of them. A few theologians can hold their own with their counterparts in the West. They are at once thoroughly Asian and thoroughly Christian. It is well known that 6,000 of about 7,000 Indian nurses are Christians. An Indian Methodist doctor in Gujarat is rapidly gaining a reputation as one of the finest surgeons of the country. In every annual conference there are in Christian service at least a few men and women of unusual endowment and spirit. It is not uncommon for preachers to forsake more lucrative employment to serve the church. Most Methodist schools have Indian principals. It is the exception for a missionary in Southern Asia to be a district superintendent. At present 57 out of a total of 64 are Indians. Their task in India is complex, many-sided, and in some respects more difficult than in the United States.

There is also evidence of creativity in the church. Several Christian artists such as Alfred D. Thomas and Frank Wesley are effective in portraying Jesus in Indian settings. College and seminary students demonstrate this quality as they enact Christian drama in the churches. They have a natural flair for the dramatic.

One enterprising village pastor solved the distressing problem of the tendency of village Christians to follow non-Christian marriage rites. He discovered that the reason was that the Christian ceremony was thought dull and brief while the Hindu marriage is exciting, colorful, and lengthy—sometimes two or three days. The Scriptures do not indicate that a Christian wedding should be dull. Indeed at the one Jesus attended, he contributed to the enlivening of the occasion. Therefore this pastor lengthened the ceremony until it stretched over a whole day. He added color, excitement, and instruction. For example, he interspersed the usual vows with hymn singing, which the villager loves, and with little sermons on the Christian home, the care of children, family worship, cleanliness. He allowed plenty of group participation. Soon there was no resorting to non-Christian rites in the villages he served.

Aside from these assets the church has a splendid heritage; Christians have good reputation in most communities. There is a tradition of co-operation among the churches that the West might properly envy. The church, not least the Methodist Church, is well organized. Julius Richter observes that our polity is "calculated to attract native Christians to take a larger share in the work of the church." [2]

The church in Southern Asia has a high regard for what might be called spiritual "tone." It insists that its missionaries be thoroughly devoted to Christ. Retreats and camp meetings are well attended. At a Methodist camp meeting at Dharur in South India a village layman, holding a dry leaf in one hand and a green leaf in the other, gave this testimony: "When I came, I was like this (holding out the dry leaf); as I go home, I am like this (extending the other)."

When we are discouraged about the church in Southern Asia, we may recall the abundant evidence that it is, after all, *His* church and take heart.

[2] *History of Missions in India,* Julius Richter, Fleming H. Revell Co., New York, 1908, p. 433.

The Typical Congregation

What has already been said will suggest that the typical congregation of Pakistan or India is to be found in a village. There are numerous Methodist churches to be found in many cities and larger towns; in fact, in seventeen of the twenty largest cities in the two lands.[3] Some of these services are conducted in English, and worship in them is not greatly different from that in a Methodist church on Main Street in almost any town in the United States. Except for language difference, worship in a vernacular urban church would not be particularly strange to the American visitor.

The village is a different matter. In the whole subcontinent are 750,000 villages, ranging in size from possibly a dozen families to as many as a thousand. In some areas they are widely scattered. In others, as in parts of Uttar Pradesh, from one village one can see other villages at every point of the compass. There behind walls of mud, or brick or stone or palm-leaf, lives India—the heart of India. In many, the gospel has never been preached. In most, no Christian congregation exists. The thought so often occurs to one that in such villages the scene is not too foreign to the world in which Jesus lived. In many respects *they* are prepared to understand the Biblical background better than we.

Critics sometimes complain that the church is too Western. This is not true of a village congregation in Southern Asia. It is thoroughly indigenous. This is true of surroundings, of language, of dress, possibly of architecture, of musical instruments, and of music, and frequently of the framework of worship and of the offering in kind—of grain or fruit or fowl.

---

[3] The stress on the village church in this section is not to deny the importance of the urban church, but only to acquaint the reader with the less familiar. The commanding position of cities in the expansion of the church is pertinent today as in St. Paul's day. Most institutions are located in cities, but the program needs to be improved with respect to more institutional churches with seven-day-a-week activities, social work, etc. Attention is being given also to new industrial areas now developing.

Yet the setting will be unmistakably Christian. Possibly a white flag bearing a cross will fly from a tree marking the Christian sector. On some doorsills appears the sign of the cross. This identifies the inhabitants. It sometimes *protects* them during period of strife between other religious groups and at all times *proclaims* the heart of a new-found faith. Strangely familiar names often strike one's ear—Isaiah, Haggai, Nehemiah, Miriam, Esther, John—names out of the Scriptures. Parents of one Methodist family bear the names of Adam and Eve. They appear to have reproduced something very like the primeval family. These names are at least Asian. Not so the Winston Churchills and Abraham Lincolns one meets in villages. Happily this trend to Western names is rapidly fading away. Thoroughly Indian names—Krupa, Lila, Aziz, Roshan —are beautiful and no less Christian.

If the occasion is at all a festival one, the visitor will be met at the edge of the village, garlanded with flowers, and conducted to the place of worship, often to the accompaniment of flutes and drums. One Methodist bishop from a Southern state was piped into town to the tune of "Marching through Georgia!" One is saluted with the greeting *"Jaya Christ!"* ("Victory to Christ!") Or the shout, "To the Lord Jesus Christ, the King, be victory!" rends the air.

A glimpse into a Methodist home may reveal a humble setting indeed. If it should be a Santal village, the house will be spotless and freshly coated with a layer of white earth. The walls may be decorated with Biblical scenes, painted with homemade pigments—visual education! In such a village the kitchen will be a clean little house separated from the rest of the living quarters. More likely it will be one room. Possessions are few. On the wall one is sure to find a picture somewhat like one from a calendar. If the inhabitants are fortunate, it will be a Christian picture; if not it may be of a Hindu deity!

In a corner just above floor level will be a tiny fireplace; a chimney will be the exception. The cooking pots, the wife's proudest possessions, will be brightly polished. Near by is an earthen vessel with a cross marked on one side—the "pot of hope" or "pot of blessing"—into which a handful of grain can be thrown as the meal is prepared. This grain is for the church.

Toward evening it is time for worship, which is held daily in many regions. Very often there will be no church building. It will come in time. As one villager said at a church dedication: "We haven't had a church yet, but there's been one in my heart."

In some parts of the country a wonderful "epidemic" of church building has broken out! The village Christians supply labor and materials for building the walls; the roof, windows, and doors are supplied by special gifts from America. What more attractive co-operative project in church-building could be conceived? Dozens of such churches now are in use in India and Pakistan. In one district alone during 1954 fourteen new houses of worship were constructed. In each of two adjoining districts five new churches have gone up. One enterprising missionary, the Rev. David A. Seamands, has started a "church factory" where trusses, windows, and doors can be put together economically in one central place.

In one village a number of Christian homes had been destroyed by fire. They decided to build a church first. "Never mind our homes—we'll rebuild them somehow," they said. "First we must think about our Church!" In another place the most desirable site for a church was already occupied by the house of a layman. He invited his friends to tear down his house. Six weeks later he had a new house in another location, and the Christians had a beautiful new red-stone church. Still another group, months after completing their new church, testified: "Do you know something? God has taken care of us as never before. We have more work, more to eat, and are all more prosperous than ever before . . . We've gone ahead on faith, and God has proved himself faithful." In one instance the Muslims of a community gave seven hundred rupees toward building a chapel. A proprietor of a liquor shop said: "Ever since these people started building a church, my business has been very, very poor." And soon he was out of business altogether.

If there is no building, a space under a tree will do. Or during the monsoon rains, perhaps a stable. After all, Jesus was born in one. If it is the former, the women will sweep the ground clean and possibly with sticks draw lines to form a kind of checkerboard. One person sits within each square, presenting an orderly worship. The pastor or a layman seats himself before the group beside a wooden cross. Much of the service may be sung. Especially do they like to join in *bhajans,* lyrical hymns. If the leader is gifted, a *kirtan* may be held— alternate preaching and singing of impromptu hymns based on a portion of Scripture. This may go on far into the night, accompanied by drums, little cymbals, castinets, or clapping of hands.

The church in India and Pakistan has been enriched by a number of fine Christian poets, so that in many areas one scarcely ever hears the singing of a translated hymn from the West. One of the greatest of these was N. V. Tilak, the great Marathi poet, a sweet singer of India. One of his translated hymns reads:

> Tenderest Mother-Guru[*] mine,
> Saviour, where is love like Thine?
>
> A cool and never-fading shade
> To souls by sin's fierce heat dismayed:
>
> Right swiftly at my earliest cry
> He came to save me from the sky:

---

[*] *Guru* means master. The phrase "Mother-Guru" may be strange, even a little offensive to us, but stressing the parental or family aspect of our relationship to Jesus, it is very meaningful to India.

> He made Him friends of those that mourn
> With hearts by meek contrition torn:
>
> For me, a sinner, yea, for me
> He hastened to the bitter Tree:
>
> And still within me living, too,
> He fills my being through and through.
>
> My heart is all one melody—
> "Hail to Thee, Christ! all hail to Thee!" [5]

In some villages one sees devotional dancing. This is most impressive. The rhythmic movements of a group of men or boys or girls is in time with their singing. The themes of the songs are invitation to worship, or evangelistic, or having to do with the great Christian festivals. The title of one such song is translated: "This is my witness: Jesus is the Son of God." Another bears the refrain: "The love of Jesus; don't forget it." Then the stanzas recall incidents in His life expressing His love. Thus through a delightful and reverent medium from their own cultural background, worship is carried on and the truths of our faith confirmed in their hearts.

A clever village preacher may illustrate his talks by references to Kabir, the outcaste mystic of the 15th century, beloved of both Muslims and Hindus, indeed of all Indians, Examples of his sayings are:

> "You steal an anvil and give a needle,
> Then mount a pedestal to await a chariot to take you to heaven."

or

> "I laugh when I see the thirsty fish in the pond,
> And I laugh when men go on pilgrimage to find God."

---

[5] *Narayan Vaman Tilak,* J. C. Winslow, Association Press, Calcutta, 1923, p. 91.

Or a pastor may illustrate evangelism by likening it to the banyan tree, familiar to his hearers, which spreads out its branches and then from the branches come further roots down into the soil. Surely the village church is indigenous! In thousands of such villages the transforming task of the gospel goes on.

An incident symbolic of this transformation occurred during World War II. Two American officers in Assam went from the airfields used to fly supplies across the "Hump" to China to a town in the mountains called Cherrapunji. Cherrapunji is famous as the wettest spot in the world. It often rains as much as 600 inches in one year. On the day of this visit it rained! They stopped their jeep on a jungle road near by. Out of the jungle came two little children of a local tribe. In the pouring rain they sang to the Americans. The song was at that time popular. It was "Pistol Packin' Mama." The officers knew that the G.I.'s had been to that out-of-the-way place, for they had taught that song to children all over India. We are all inevitably missionaries! Inevitably sharing!

These visitors also learned that Christian missionaries had been to Cherrapunji. The Baptists, curiously enough, failed to establish a station at the wettest spot in the world! But the Welsh Presbyterians had evangelized effectively, for 80 per cent of the tribesmen were Christians. Some of them, formerly headhunters had been trained as choirs to sing the "Hallelujah Chorus." Such is the Christian's tranforming task!

That anthem will never be sung properly until it is joined in by people of every nation, kindred, tongue, and people. Since we are necessarily missionary, we can share the worst we have or the best we have. And the best we have is Jesus!

CHAPTER II

SET AMID PERPLEXITIES

THE WELL-KNOWN prayer, "For the Church," by Walter Rauschenbusch begins: "O God, we pray for thy Church, which is set today amid the perplexities of a changing order, and face to face with a great new task." [1] This petition is particularly pertinent to the church in Southern Asia. An understanding of the "changing order" will suggest something of the "great new task" there and will serve at the same time as a gateway for insights regarding the church in India and Pakistan today.

Much that is said about one of these countries can be said about the other. At the same time their divergencies are nowadays becoming all too apparent. They possess a great deal of history in common. They were both until 1947 one people united under British rule. Both are now engaged in the difficult and important task of nation-building. They are set amid a rapidly changing and revolutionary Asia. No longer can one speak of the "Changeless East." Nor can one say, "You cannot hurry the East," for it is moving very rapidly. Rapid change causes restlessness and confusion which may have good or bad results. One is reminded of Amos 5:19: "As if a man did flee from a lion, and a bear met him; or went into the house, and leaned his hand on the wall, and a serpent bit him." This verse would, however, do injustice to the situation in which many positive and important features are apparent. Incidentally the passage must not be understood as referring to the British lion, nor the Russian bear, nor the Indian cobra!

---

[1] From *Prayers of the Social Awakening,* by Walter Rauschenbusch, Boston: The Pilgrim Press, 1925, p. 134. Used by permission.

Set Amid History

Indians have plenty of history, and they are intensely and justifiably proud of it.

During the 1920's excavations in the Indus valley in the northwest revealed evidence of high cultures which predated the Aryan influx. The principal archaeological investigations took place in what is now Pakistan. The high point of this civilization dates from about 2500 B.C., contemporary to and rivalling developments in Egypt and Mesopotamia. Some interrelation between these areas is suggested but not clearly proved.

The Indus River people were city dwellers. Their streets were carefully laid out; they had good drainage systems; pottery was a highly developed art. Their brick houses were often of several storeys, complete with baths. They had the wheel; bovine animals, but not horses; they had mastered writing. They were doubtless aboriginal dwellers of India, called Dravidian after their language. Moreover, they show evidence of religious practices which formerly were supposed to have been imported by the Aryans. Actually Hinduism would seem historically to be a mingling of the Aryan religion with that already present.

About 1500 B.C. the nomadic Aryans entered from the north, from the steppes of Central Asia. They were herdsmen and agriculturists. They spoke a form of Sanskrit. Other branches of these people went westward into Europe; hence, the kinship of Indo-Germanic languages. They had the horse; they venerated the cow; their religion was elaborate and abounded in nature interest. They moved gradually into the river valleys of northern India, subduing, subjecting, and to a degree intermingling with the earlier inhabitants.

Indians are proud, too, of their fellow countryman, the first Buddha—Gautama (563-483 B.C.). A nobleman of the second or warrior caste, he founded a religion which was one of the many protests of his period against the ritualistic, priest-ridden Hinduism. His was a moderate approach in contrast to the extreme asceticism, on the one hand, contrived by the Jains, and atheistic materialism which was on the other hand advocated by some reformers. Hence Buddhism is called the religion of "the Middle Way."

The most famous of the Buddhist rulers was Asoka of the 3rd century B.C. His was a highly progressive and successful reign during which a great portion of the Indian peninsula was unified. Such unity was only attained two other times: under the Moghal emperor, Akbar, a contemporary of Queen Elizabeth I, and during the modern Anglo-Indian period.

India has been likened to a low-pressure area on a weather map, into which winds blow: so India has attracted repeated invasions. The first clear contact with the Mediterranean world was made in 326 B.C. when Alexander the Great invaded India. Traces of Greek influence survive even yet.

The next thrust from the West was in a series of Muslim inroads beginning in the 8th century of our era. The intensity of these periodic invasions increased, reaching its height under the Moghal emperors, the first of whom came shortly after Columbus discovered America.

The third thrust of the West was from modern European nations—the Portuguese, the Dutch, the French, the Danish, and the more successful British. With the latter the stage is set for modern developments. Though all these invasions had their military aspects, they also involved cultural penetration to which India's culture had to react.

The British Connection

India "enjoyed" nearly 350 years of association with the British. Queen Elizabeth I gave a charter to the London East India Company on December 31, 1600. During the century that followed they developed trading ports or "factories" at various harbors around the Indian coast—Madras, Calcutta, Bombay. Other European nations had similar establishments.

It was not until about the time of the American Revolution that Britain began to consolidate her position politically. Lord Cornwallis after Yorktown became the second Governor-General of India and helped to consolidate British rule there. Gradually political control supplanted the largely commercial aims of the East India Company until the latter was abolished altogether after the Indian Mutiny (1857). It later became a rather sad aphorism of Indian nationalists that "the English conquered India using manpower furnished by the Indians." Tens of millions came to be ruled by a handful of British, possibly never exceeding 100,000 in number.

Christian Missions entered India in spite of the East India Company. No Christian Indians were allowed to be company officials. Hindu temples and Muslim mosques were often subsidized. When Wilberforce in 1792 pleaded with the directors for "missionaries and schoolmasters," they replied that "the Hindus had as good a system of faith and morals as most people, and that it would be madness to attempt their conversion or to give them any more learning . . . than that which they already possessed." [1]

All along the British were officially neutral toward religions. British officers often privately supported missionary effort, but the British connection was not used to further the Christian enterprise. Furthermore, the conduct of many foreigners was a scandal to Christianity.

What galled India's people, especially in the latter years, was the air of superiority which the average Englishman adopted toward them. It was this contempt which was at the root of the inevitable resistance. At the same time the Indians had a tremendous admiration for the British, if for no other reason than the latter's ability to subject them to docile rule. Indians borrowed much from the West. This fact, mingled with intense

---

[1] Quoted by Arthur Mayhew: *"The Education of India,"* Faber and Gwyer, London, 1926, p. 10.

pride in their own culture, set up a tension in the Indian mind which has continued even since independence. It accounts for some of the Indian's extreme sensitiveness.

Indian nationalist sentiment began to gather force about the middle of the last century. The abortive and bloody attempt to overthrow foreign rule in 1857 is well known in history and fiction. Termed by English writers, the Mutiny, Indian historians regard it as "the first War for Independence."

The most potent political group which finally won independence was the Indian National Congress. Founded in 1885 by an Englishman, Allan Octavian Hume, it was originally a rather mild and polite political debating society. It commanded interest from many religious groups, though predominantly Hindu. In the early years of the present century the Congress began to agitate for dominion status like Canada. Finally its aim sharpened to complete severance from Britain. On January 26, 1930, Congress declared India independent, though as in our own history, it took several years to realize that goal.

A great Indian nationalist, Tilak, said: "*Swaraj* (home rule) is my birthright, and I will have it!" This became a battle cry. George Bernard Shaw pointed out once with regard to India that a man without his freedom was like a man with cancer: "he could think of nothing else."

By the middle 1940's it would be fair to say that all major groups in Indian life wanted freedom—Congress, orthodox Hindus, Muslims, moderates, and the Princes—but their definition of freedom would have been qualified in various ways. Even the British overlords could point to a mounting series of declarations of intent to allow home rule. Increasingly government responsibility was shared with Indians, who nevertheless retained doubts about the ultimate sincerity of British promises of full freedom.

Undoubtedly the fulfillment of nationalist aims was greatly hastened by the leadership of Mahatma (Great Soul) Gandhi. He devised a technique of agitation peculiarly suited to the

Indian people. He called it *satyagraha* (truth-force), and his program, finally successful, was termed "nonviolent noncooperation." During this period going to jail was regarded as a badge of honor. Nehru himself spent fourteen years in prison. For Indians, Gandhi is regarded as the "Father of his Country." Not only did he win freedom but prepared his people for it, contributing to national unity (except for Muslims), self-respect, morale, and morality.

Having thus briefly described the course of modern Indian nationalism, it is necessary to state that in the main Christian Indians did not take a major part in the struggle. There were, of course, notable exceptions, such as the fine Christian patriots, K. T. Paul, H. C. Mukherji, S. K. Datta, to mention only a few. Missionaries were by legal agreement, if not almost by definition, neutral in the national struggle—again with notable exceptions. Dr. E. Stanley Jones was one such exception. Indian Christians have often held that they were restrained by missionaries and encouraged to remain aloof from the national movement. There was just enough truth in this aloofness to seem to lend justification to the mistaken idea that to become a Christian was to be denationalized and to make credible the slanderous remark that Christians were the "running dogs of imperialism."

A special word about Pakistan is necessary. British rule supplanted the last of the Moghal emperors after 1857. The Muslim had made a great and enriching contribution to the synthesis of Indian culture. After 1857 there was a kind of sullen withdrawal of Muslims from public life. On the other hand, their great reformer, Sir Syed Ahmed Khan (1817-1899), spent his efforts to arouse and modernize Muslim outlook. He founded the famous Muslim University at Aligarh and was responsible for a great renascence of Indian Islam. In 1906 the Muslim League was founded to care for the community interests. For some years this organization worked in fairly close harmony with the Indian National Congress.

Pakistan means literally "land of the pure." It first of all expressed a religious concept. The name is said to have been coined by an Indian Muslim student in England and was popularized by the famous Muslim poet, the late Muhammed Iqbal, during the 1930's. It remained, however, for the strong-minded and polished lawyer, Mahomed Ali Jinnah, to conceive of Pakistan in practical political terms and by iron determination to achieve it. His compatriots regard him as the father of his country and termed him, Quaid-i-Azam or Great Leader.

Under Jinnah's guidance, the Muslim League passed in 1940 the famous Lahore Resolution calling for the goal of Pakistan. He propounded a "Two-Nation Theory," that Hindus and Muslims could not be one people. Although the Congress leaders bore the brunt of the struggle for freedom, Jinnah and his associates were insistent on partition of the subcontinent. Pakistan celebrates Independence on August 14; India, the day following. Though the goal of a homeland for Indian Muslims was secured, yet the Hindu-Muslim problem was not solved; for about 35,000,000 Muslims remain in India.

Evaluation of British rule depends on one's point of view. Some moderate Indians such as the late Justice Ranade of Bombay saw their coming as providential. Nehru has acknowledged the debt for the heritage of Western science they introduced. At the same time he has stated that the poorest parts of India are precisely those where the British had been the longest.

The British brought about political unity; they preserved peace; they set up an efficient political administration, including public services of education and public health. The nationalist would reply that "good government is no substitute for self-government." He would advance the assertion that India was one-third literate in 1800 and one-sixth literate in 1900. Britain introduced modern technology and industry. The Indian would reply that India in reality fell behind Western industry during foreign rule; that Japan was more thoroughly industrialized without outside domination. Britain gained in commerce, defense bases, prestige, experience in colonial rule, in positions for her young men. It was not without cause that India was called the "brightest gem in the imperial crown."

British rule was on the whole benevolent; it was voluntarily surrendered; India and Pakistan did have good tutelage as they emerged into modern times as democracies.

Set Amid Revolution

India and Pakistan are set today amid Asia in revolution. We tend to hold the word "revolution" in suspicion because it often connotes violent upheaval and change. In the context of the American Revolution, for instance, we do not object to the word. Until the 17th century revolution was not used as a political term at all; rather with respect to astronomy—the revolving of the heavenly spheres. It has now come down to earth and is very much with us!

Some regard communism as the basic moving force or dynamic of Asia. This is not primarily so. Rather, the dynamic is a threefold expression of basic urges. One is the urge for freedom, especially political freedom. Another is the urge for the better life, defined in quite material terms—better food, better clothing, better wages, better housing, better opportunity for one's children. The third is the urge for equality. Asians are tired of being regarded as second-class people. Nehru once said: "Yesterday Asia was a prey. Today it is a power. Tomorrow it will be an even greater power." In varying degree these three legitimate urges can be applied to any land of Asia today. They apply to Africa as well. By understanding them we can have an insight into what of importance is going on in these areas today.

There are some corollaries to these urges. (1) The achievement of freedom does not necessarily carry with it the achievement of the better life and equality. India and Pakistan are illustrations of this and are striving valiantly toward these other goals. (2) The converse is true: pursuit of the better life and equality does not necessarily carry with it freedom. China illustrates this, appearing to have lost much of her freedom. (3) Christians have a responsibility for awakening these urges. We have preached a gospel that all men are of value and are equal in the sight of God. They want to be equal in the sight of other men! We have declared that their true role and destiny is as sons of the living God. This awakens demands in the human breast which must be satisfied. (4) Once these legitimate desires are awakened, the Communists with specious promises of fulfillment tend to corrupt them.

In such a situation, Christians, East and West, are called upon to recover a sense of revolution themselves. It is easy for us to be maneuvered into a position of opposing legitimate social revolution. What is more revolutionary than a faith which declares men can be born anew? What is more revolutionary than the leaven which can transform the whole? What is more revolutionary than the faith which could once be said to have "turned the world upside down"?

This revolution is asserting itself strongly in the realm of ideas. One of these is a vigorous sense of nationalism. Nationalism is a Western disease, highly contagious in Asia. In Europe nationalism developed in a positive sense, as the expression of common language and culture. In Asia it has developed in a more virulent form—protest against Western imperialism and colonialism. It was coupled with deep resentment of economic exploitation and racial difference. Freedom having been attained, the other resentments continue to smolder with certain forces ready to fan them into flame.

Once political freedom is established, nationalism tends to develop around other rallying centers; for example, religion. So much has been borrowed from the Western world that an effort is made to preserve the soul of the culture—religion—intact. This was true of Japan in the development of state Shinto and emperor worship. Thus the tendency in Southern Asia on the part of some is to make religion the test for citizenship: Islam in Pakistan and Hinduism in India. It can only be hoped that more reasonable elements in these lands will continue to prevail.

Why Should Americans be Interested?

A student at Lucknow Christian College said, "You Americans ought to be interested in us; for, after all, when Columbus discovered you, he was looking for us!" He was merely giving expression to the great community of interest between us.

This community of interest has economic facets. These countries have raw materials that America greatly needs. Moreover many American firms are establishing or expanding their plants in Southern Asia. These include Socony Vacuum, Firestone, Otis Elevator, and Union Carbide, to mention only a few. We need each other economically.

There are also intellectual facets. Numbers of Indian and Pakistani students study in the United States. There is considerable interchange of ideas. It is often forgotten that India ranks third among the nations respecting the number of citizens who speak English; first America, then Britain, then India.

India drew largely from the U. S. Constitution in framing her own. As independence drew near, the U. S. Information Service libraries in the subcontinent had a heavy demand on books regarding early American history.

Our lives are interrelated. An American missionary was walking along a fairly remote, narrow road in the Himalayas. A jeep came quickly by, almost brushing him off the road. It stopped and its driver proved to be a fellow American. He was from the U. S. Department of Agriculture, hunting the natural enemies of the Himalayan fruit-fly. It seems that this pest had found its way to our shores on an army transport during World War II. It was affecting the fruit crops of Hawaii and California. He sought its natural insect enemies that it might be brought under control.

We ought to be interested, for India alone represents the

largest free nation of our world. Dr. John R. Mott visiting India in 1953 said, "India is supremely important to us now. Human destiny as a whole may be determined by decisions which are in the making here." Supreme Court Justice William O. Douglas stated during a recent visit to Australia that India "was on the march up through the ranks of the democratic world . . . one of the really bright spots in the world today.[2]

We ought to be interested in India for it, together with Pakistan, is the testing ground of democracy in Asia today. A group of Methodists were visiting the White House early in the Eisenhower administration. After speaking to the visitors, the President called upon one who had a background of service in India to state in one sentence what was significant there. Quite an assignment! In substance the reply was that "in Asia were two great land areas, India and China; both were confronted with the same complex problems; China was trying to solve them by the coercive methods of communism; India was trying to solve them by voluntary democratic methods." Much depends on the outcome. If democracy should fail in India, it will likely fail throughout Asia and the 700,000,000 uncommitted Asians may be forced into the other camp. Then the whole balance in the world would be thrown off. The plight of the remaining democracies would then be grave indeed.

We ought to be interested in Indians and Pakistanis, for there are so many of them. India's 360,000,000 alone represent more people than are in all of the twenty-two nations in the Western Hemisphere combined.

We ought to be interested in these people because of what they can be. Nearly fifty years ago when E. Stanley Jones first went to India, he said that the India of that day could be summed up in one word: *paralysis*. India then was paralyzed. Today the word is *potentiality,* and it can be applied to almost every aspect of life in Pakistan and India.

---

[2] Quoted by Newcastle, Australia, *Sun,* July 21, 1954.

We ought to be interested in these two lands, for we have much to share. The world cannot be stable with one part of it enjoying an overabundance and other parts in abysmal need. The United States has about 7 percent of the world's population and more than half of the world's income. Those figures stand in judgment upon us!

We need each other. In May, 1953, Mt. Everest was conquered. But it took a representative of Western culture, Hillary, and a representative of Asia, Tensing, to do it. Many other moral and spiritual Everests remain; possibly if we work together, they too can be overcome.

Earnest Christians will be interested in these lands. For we are commanded to love all, to be neighbors to all, to serve all. We are commanded to declare and demonstrate the Gospel everywhere and to share with others what we ourselves prize most.

The United States and Southern Asia

Between Pakistan and the United States relations are mutually cordial. This was shown in the gift of wheat to Pakistan in 1953. Extensive aid was rendered in the flood disaster of the summer of 1954 in East Pakistan, followed by considerable economic aid. May, 1954, saw the signing of a military aid agreement between the two countries. This cordiality stems partly from the fact that a "meeting of minds" is easier between Western and Islamic nations than between the former and India. Partly it is due to a different heritage of relationship to the Indian struggle for independence; Pakistan's separate existence was determined late in the day without Pakistan's present-day leaders having been very much involved in gaining freedom from the British. Partly, it is due to the fact that those very leaders feel that it is in the national interest to be closely related to the West.

In the case of India, United States relations are correct enough; still misunderstanding each of the other exists in both lands. It is true that neither country enjoys a "good press" in the other country. On a person to person basis, however, the American in India is treated with friendliness and courtesy. There is often an anti-*America* attitude there, with reference to some particular policy; there is not a strong anti-*American* attitude, with respect to people.

As Americans we do well to be as objective as possible about this. We like to be liked. It is hard for us to endure criticism. Indians, too, are sensitive, a tendency enhanced by her experience of foreign domination. They resent deeply any condescending attitude; the repetition of the standard clichés about her— that India is a land of wonder and mystery; that Indians are either fabulously wealthy or degradingly poor. It is perhaps evidence of immaturity on both sides that criticism cannot be accepted in better grace.

Our two countries disagree in attitude toward China. India has recognized the present government of China, but so have Pakistan, Great Britain, New Zealand, Sweden, and a dozen other countries. That fact in itself is no basis for forsaking friendship for India. She argues that diplomatic recognition does not imply approval of form of government.

India and America differ also in attitude toward international communism. We feel that India is "soft" toward Communist nations. Indians feel that Americans can see no other evils such as colonialism from which she herself so recently emerged. They feel that some way must be found to get along with these nations. Nehru says that it is either "co-existence" or "co-extinction." It is for this reason that India refused to join in the Southeast Asia Treaty Organization.

India resents our military aid to Pakistan. She thinks it will upset the balance of power in Southern Asia; that it may involve economic imperialism in the region on the part of the United States. Furthermore she regards it unfriendly on our part to "take sides" when the two neighboring countries are involved in disputes.

The United States feels that Nehru freely criticizes the democracies but not the communist bloc of nations. India replies that she can afford to be quite frank with friendly fellow democracies but cannot take so much liberty with the other bloc. On occasion Nehru has criticized Russia; for example, when he opposed further H-bomb tests, he addressed his complaint both to Russia and to the United States.

India was hurt by not being asked to the Geneva Conference in 1954. The United States opposed her participating, for she had not sent troops to fight in Korea. (She did send an ambulance unit.) India thought that a settlement in Asia was a legitimate concern of hers as the largest free Asian nation. Her role as an agent in bringing about a Korean armistice; her supervision of prisoner exchange; her good offices which aided in an Indo-China cease-fire—she hopes may be recognized as conciliatory.

Americans often think of India taking a radically different line of approach to that of the United States in the United Nations. Sometimes this is true. In 1951, however, Mme. Pandit, later President of the United Nations, reported that in recent sessions of the United Nations General Assembly India had voted with the United States thirty-eight out of fifty-one times, abstained eleven times, and differed only twice. In the 1952-53 General Assembly the two disagreed on only one out of thirty-six issues.

Sometimes we complain about India's foreign policy. Historically it is not very different from our own. Basically it is one not of neutrality but non-alignment or non-involvement—not lining up specifically with either power bloc—and judging each issue on its own merits. The United States was isolationist until very recent years; there is still much American sentiment of that persuasion. India is almost precisely where we were as a nation when George Washington advised us against "entangling alliances," so that we might during our early years concentrate on internal development. As we by our Monroe

Doctrine oppose outside interference in this hemisphere, so India does not like outside interference in Southern Asia. India is sympathetic to other nations under colonial rule as, indeed, we are. She favors action through the United Nations, on which policy we are agreed. In common with us also she is opposed to aggression, communist or otherwise, and in good Gandhian tradition seeks for peace. Our fear of India being in any sense "on the fence" is essentially a lack of confidence in the ways of democracy—that they are not attractive enough for her to come down on the right side!

It is probably true that much of the resentment from India, formerly attached to the British, has ironically since Independence been transferred to the United States. This is almost inevitable with respect to the richest and most powerful nation in the world.

What then is an American to do? For one thing he can benefit by seeing himself through the eyes of others. He can recognize the importance of having friendly critics. He can afford to be patient.

Prime Minister Nehru understands us perhaps better than most Americans understand him. He said in 1951:

"I went to the United States a year and a half ago. I knew something about American people. I had read their history, their Constitution, their progress, their literature, so I looked forward to that visit very greatly. I went there, and saw large numbers of people in many fields; I saw many famous places. And the more I remained in America, and the more people I saw, the more I got the impression of an essential friendliness, of frankness, of forthrightness—qualities that I value very greatly—and I returned with the feeling of great friendship and gratitude for America and her people."

They Have Problems

Go for a moment to a part of North India called the Terai. It is a jungly, swampy, malaria-ridden region at the foot of the Himalayas. The mosquito has in the past defeated efforts to reclaim the land. Now with DDT and other malaria-control measures the land is being recovered. Two great caterpillar tractors advance through the jungle, an anchor chain between them. This fells the trees, sweeping the jungle clear. Bulldozers push the trees together; some lumber is recovered; scrub is burned. Then great rakes digging four feet into the soil cut the roots; then the plowing; then the planting; then the harvest. Christians are interested in such land redemption, as in every other form of redemption.

At this place one day visitors were told of an invasion of wild elephants, trampling to the ground acres of the new sugar-cane crop. As the visitors went out at night to see wildlife, they were asked not to shoot any tigers or leopards. Upon inquiring why, they were told: "They're our friends. At night the deer come out of the mountains to eat our crops. The tigers and leopards keep down the deer population!"

We do well to remember these incidents. The sugar-cane farmers in our South do not have to worry about wild elephants trampling their crops. Nor do U. S. farmers have to worry too much about deer; not at all about tigers and leopards lurking in the night. In other words, the people of these lands are striving valiantly toward solving their problems (land reclamation is one such effort) but contend with odds of which we have little conception. They demand our sympathy and patience.

These two countries have a multitude of problems: poverty, illiteracy, disease, too many people *on* the land, too little production *from* the land (eight bushels of wheat per acre, sixty eggs per hen annually), too little industrial production, too much reproduction, factors of disunity, under-employment of educated people, problems of character, problems of millions of refugees. These problems and many others are confronting Indians and Pakistanis all at once. Recently Prime Minister Nehru wearily told an American educator: "How can we think of education when only 20 percent of India's people have enough to eat; 40 percent have inadequate food; 40 percent positively deficient, to the point of starvation?" Look at it in this perspective: the

United States has been independent nearly one hundred and seventy-five years; we started with a virgin soil; with a population of only 1 percent of that of present-day Southern Asia; we had plenty of time to work on the problems, with a vigorous, select people, in a comparatively isolated world. Pakistan and India, free since 1947 in old, tired, thickly populated regions find themselves faced with an array of difficulties and the whole world looking "over their shoulders," not necessarily cheering for their success.

Both countries are working on these problems. For example, though in Islam women have traditionally an inferior position, progress is being registered in improving their status. As a symbol, during 1954 the first Muslim woman ambassador, the widow of the late Prime Minister Liaquat Ali Khan, was assigned to the Netherlands. Another Pakistani woman was included among her country's representatives at the United Nations. In India, too, age-old prejudice is being slowly overcome. The famous Hindu philosopher, now vice-president of India, Dr. S. Radhakrishnan, recently said: "Caste must go." A Hindu minister of agriculture in one of the states: "We must get rid of unfit cattle." Though monkeys are still widely revered, bounties of two rupees are offered for monkey tails in one state; five rupees for a pelt in another.

Both countries are working hard on the problem of land redistribution. The various states have taken the initiative in this difficult and important matter and not the central government. India's constitution has been amended to allow for land reform. Nearly all the states have passed the necessary legislation. In general the aim is to give ownership of land to the one who actually tills it, thus setting aside the ancient landlord system, so often oppressive. A ceiling is put on the amount of land any one person can hold. Compensation is paid to the former owner, usually by the government. The cultivator repays the government over a period of years. Progress, however, is slow and meets with considerable resistance.

A unique voluntary scheme of land redistribution in India is going forward under the leadership of Acharya Vinoba Bhave. This ascetic figure, a disciple of Gandhi, walks barefooted around the country asking landholders to give him land free for parcelling out to the poor. It is called *Bhoodan Yagna* or "Land Gift Movement." He whimsically terms it "looting with love." His goal is to receive 50,000,000 acres by 1957, one sixth of the arable land of the country. By mid-1955 he had collected about 4,000,000 acres. In a land-hungry nation, this procedure is something of an indigenous answer to communism which often glibly promises land for the peasant.

The depth to which political leaders feel these problems is seen in this statement from Nehru: "There is no complete freedom as long as there is starvation, hunger, lack of clothing, lack of necessities of life, lack of opportunities for growth for a single human being, man, woman and child, in this country." Christians can feel no less deeply about it as followers of One who came that men might have life abundantly.

One of the deepest problems is that of interrelations between India and Pakistan. Unfortunately since Independence relations have not gone smoothly. Partition of the subcontinent was a bitter experience for Indians who called it "vivisection." Almost immediately after transfer of authority from the British, certain lawless elements broke into fighting and rioting. In Pakistan Muslims set upon their Hindu and Sikh neighbors. On the other side of the border unruly groups of Hindus and Sikhs attacked Muslims. It was from this situation that there resulted the mass migration of five to seven millions of people each way across the borders between the two countries, Muslims from India and Sikhs and Hindus from Pakistan. This was the greatest such migration in history. Just how many met violent death or died from hardship from the experience no one knows, but they numbered in the tens of thousands. Memories of such occurrences die slowly and serve to fan the flames of disagreement between India and Pakistan.

There are three main areas of disagreement—over Kashmir, over refugee property, over canal water. Kashmir was a native state, a spot of beauty in the Himalayas, reaching up into central Asia. The fabulous Vale of Kashmir is the central fertile valley of the state; the Persian poets called it an "emerald set in pearls"—a green valley surrounded by snow-capped mountains. In the autumn of 1947 tribesmen raided the state from the northwest of Pakistan. The Maharajah, whose small army could not defend the area, decided to unite with India and ask for protection of the Indian Army. Its troops were flown in, and later the Pakistan regular army joined in the fighting. India appealed to the United Nations Security Council.

Later, January 1, 1949, a cease-fire was brought into force which has been respected ever since. Pakistan claims the state because the majority of the inhabitants are Muslims. India states that it has many Muslim citizens, too, and besides it is a secular state with equal right for all, regardless of religion. Legally the state is hers by accession of the Maharajah. What the outcome will be no one knows. Perhaps a long-delayed plebiscite will award it to one or another country; perhaps a partition may be agreed upon; perhaps the stalemate will continue and finally the present cease-fire lines will be recognized as permanent borders.

Refugee property settlement is also difficult. Simply stated, many of the refugees from Pakistan to India were business and professional people who left much behind. Muslim refugees from India to Pakistan were mainly farmers or farm laborers. Thus any settlement of property losses would involve a large payment by Pakistan to India, which the former is reluctant to make.

As to canal waters, there is a great deal of irrigation in West Pakistan. Several of the rivers supplying water to the canals pass through India to Pakistan. Thus if India withdraws too much water, her neighbor suffers sorely. The World Bank has offered its good offices to settle the dispute. The solution suggested is for the water of three rivers to be used mainly by India. The other three principal rivers will be for Pakistan's use. It appears that both countries will finally accept this solution.

They Have Plans

Both countries have plans for economic improvement. Pakistan has a six-year Development Program which involves over a hundred separate plans calling for the expenditure of about $700,000,000. Primary attention is being given to industrialization, especially of types that will in turn benefit rural economy. Though the world's largest jute (burlap) producer, Pakistan at Partition had no jute mills. Also a producer of hides, cotton, wool and silk, she had few plants to process these products. More factories are contemplated. During 1953 the world's largest jute plant was opened in East Pakistan. In addition, several hydro-electric schemes are under construction; chemical and food production plants are being built; and a major natural gas field is being brought into use in West Pakistan.

In India a more elaborate Five Year Plan was launched on April 1, 1952. It contemplates an expenditure of approximately $4,500,000,000. Something over three fourths of this amount is in sight. First priority is given to the increase of food production. To this end irrigation is being expanded, and a score or more multi-purpose hydro-electric dam projects are at various stages of construction. Even before Independence India had irrigation canals enough to reach three times around the earth, or as Lord Wavell once said, "six times around Mars," where fabled canals are supposed to exist! It also aims at increasing industrial production of both light and heavy types; at enlarging transport facilities, communications of all kinds; rehabilitation of refugees; rural development; expansion of social services and education. It touches also on land reform and relief of economic inequality.

At the halfway point of the first plan, a second five-year plan was being discussed. Already impressive gains had been registered. It is immensely encouraging to drive along hundreds of miles of new black-top roads in India and to observe the many new "approach" roads to villages, often constructed with the voluntary labor of the villagers themselves. Detours are about as common as in the 1920's in the United States because of numbers of new bridges. Shops are full of many types of consumer goods. The harvests of the spring of 1954 were the largest on record. India was green and gold—ripe unto harvest! A large locomotive manufacturing plant is functioning; a new fertilizer plant produces a thousand tons per day. In addition, the International Monetary Fund states: "India has had an exceptionally successful record in combating inflation in the past few years. This is no accident at a time when prices were rising throughout the world. It is a result of a determined and intelligent credit policy."

Of special interest are the dams, organized after the Tennessee Valley Authority model. One system of six dams in the Damodar Valley, near Calcutta, will increase fivefold the cultivable land in the area; can supply power for doubling industry nearby; can vastly enhance electricity for Calcutta and its environs. In North India the Bhakra Dam will be the second highest in the world. A score of other major dam projects are at various stages of construction.

Of still more immediate importance is the Community Development Program, biggest of its type to be undertaken anywhere. On Gandhi's birthday, October 2, 1952, a total of fifty-five project areas were started, each touching about three hundred villages. This has been expanded since so that 120,000 villages in all will be receiving some sort of rural extension service of a comprehensive type involving agriculture, sanitation, education, health, and cottage industry. Results for such an ambitious program are on the whole encouraging, though some are lagging.

Aid from the United States through 1954 for various undertakings amounted to nearly $400,000,000 (including the $190,-000,000 wheat loan of 1951). Additional external help comes from countries of the Commonwealth which are involved in the Colombo Plan and from the World Bank. Most of the necessary capital is, however, being found within the country. India has, by the way, not defaulted on her repayment of loans. On the list of countries having received United States aid India stands high in proportions already paid back. She insists, however, that she will not accept aid "with strings attached."

What About Communism?

This is not the place for a detailed discussion of communism in India and Pakistan. Some attention must be given it, however, if for no other reason than the easy assumption on the part of many that because China has turned to communism, Southern Asia must inevitably do the same.

The undoubted interest of Russia in this region must be acknowledged frankly. There is the oft-quoted saying of Lenin that "for World Communism the road to Paris lies through Peking and Calcutta." Doubtless the Communists have a calendar of events looking to this end. Moscow scarcely wishes to contribute to peace and stability in Asia. Methods Communists employ in Southern Asia are similar to those used elsewhere.

In Pakistan, Communists are more active in the East around the industrial and volatile city of Dacca. In India they are most evident in three sections. One is in and about Calcutta, so crowded and overtaxed as to be a breeding ground for discontent among the dispossessed. A second area is Hyderabad and Andhra States. There the oppression of feudalistic overlords was until 1948 intolerable—all the land of the former, a large state, was supposed to have been held by twenty-eight landowners. The third area was highly educated Travancore-Cochin. Land fragmentation is intense; the educated trained too much for the academic, too little for the practical. A villager there who was asked who taught him communism replied, "Mr. Stomach."

There are said to be about 100,000 Communists in India. Though Indians do not view the problem of Communism with the same intensity and urgency as Americans, the government has taken stern measures when they have engaged in violence. Leaders are fully aware of their danger internally. The "elder statesman" of India, C. Rajagopalachari, Chief Minister of Madras, addressed the Communists in the legislative assembly saying, "I place my cards on the table and tell you plainly that I am your enemy number one, and you are my enemy number one." He also said that India "must choose freedom or new Communist enslavement."

Communism is looked on with considerable disfavor by Indians because of its anti-national character. During World War II they co-operated with the British because they, in turn, were allied with Russia. Communists would now like to forget this episode, but Congress leaders will not allow them. The fact of Indian Communists taking orders from Moscow does not sit well with Indian nationalists. The banner of nationalism is still firmly in the hands of Nehru and his associates.

Nor can Indian Communists claim rightfully to be Gandhi's successors. Their deeds of violence have been a denial of this. Nor have they been able to establish their claim of being champions of the oppressed. They promised much to villagers in Hyderabad State prior to the general elections. Subsequently, unable to deliver according to their promises, some Communist leaders have had to seek police protection!

Many wonder about Mr. Nehru's attitude toward Communists. He has opposed them vigorously in Parliament where they follow the party line. He has said that communism "crushes the free spirit of man." He declares that the policy of Indian Communists is "destructive and not constructive." At a recent public meeting he stated: "The Communists' policy indicates a lack of allegiance not only to the national flag but to the conception of India itself. If you follow Communist policy, I am sure the unity of India will be shattered." When last the Prime

Minister visited Paris, the Communists there demonstrated against him. A Communist told a missionary: "We Communists are glad when American magazines are against Nehru, because he's against us."

Pakistan, for its part, outlawed communism throughout the country in May, 1954. It would be a mistake, however, to regard religion in either country as a bulwark against the Marxist virus. For one thing the "Communist line" tones down its atheistic emphasis there. For another, Communists are adept in using religious concepts to advance their own aims.

Some comparison with China is important. It should not be forgotten that the Mao regime took charge there after years of chaotic conditions; after twenty-five years of sporadic fighting by a Communist army; after China was weakened by eight years of war with Japan as well as internal breakdown and corruption. India, on the other hand, and to a degree Pakistan, have enjoyed comparative peace, a fairly smooth transfer of power after long schooling in democracy by the British. Moreover, the governments are firmly in authority throughout the lands. Communications are good; inflation is under control. There are no counterparts to the war-lords. The army is non-political and loyal. Genuine reform is in progress. Corruption is not out of hand. The Communists, thus far, lack a leader who is a challenging figure in either country.

The chances seem favorable that India will not "go Communist." If the present liberal, democratic regime is honest enough and rapidly brings sufficient relief to India's needs; if a major war can be avoided; if democracies in the West are helpful, India need not follow in the way of China. The complete routing of the Communists in the important election in Andhra State in the spring of 1955 is a hopeful sign.

CHAPTER III

"NOT OF THIS FOLD"

INDIA IS a meeting place of many religions; and where religions meet, there is a missionary situation. This is not new to the Indo-Pakistan subcontinent; for Islam, a missionary religion, has spread widely there. Moreover, Buddhism and, to a lesser degree, Hinduism long ago reached out in expansion from India. The brother of Emperor Asoka was a Buddhist missionary to Ceylon.

Popular thought conceives of the missionary serving in some remote corner of the world. Some, of course, do. The missionary is an inveterate boundary crosser, but not all the boundaries are between nations. Some are boundaries of society or of the mind. The mission of the church is to all outside its present borders. Wherever men are, to them the Christian owes a debt of testimony and service. It is not a matter of the West going to the East, nor the American to the Indian, but of the *Christian* going to *people* whatever their background may be.

"Very Religious"

St. Paul began his address in the Areopagus of Athens with the words, "Ye men of Athens, in all things I perceive that ye are very religious." The same words might be used today with respect to citizens of any city in the Indo-Pakistan subcontinent. India is a veritable laboratory of religions. Someone has termed it a "primeval forest of religions." It is not our purpose to expound these faiths fully but to give attention to the religious atmosphere surrounding the church in Southern Asia.

It is well to remember that *all* the principal living religions of the world originated in Asia—several of them in India. Nine of the world's twelve important religions are now represented in some strength there.

A visitor in Bombay during the course of a brief tour can meet adherents of each of these faiths. He would not fail to see some fellow Christians at the many Catholic and Protestant churches of the city. Passing a shop he will observe a sign bearing a strangely familiar Semitic name. It belongs to a Jew—of the Beni-Israelites whose ancestors are said to have been shipwrecked on the west coast of India centuries ago. In any part of the city he encounters men wearing fezzes, perhaps accompanied by veiled women—Muslims. On beautiful Malabar Hill he will pass the Towers of Silence where Parsees or Zoroastrians dispose of their dead by exposure to the birds. Nearby is a fire-temple of that faith and outside its doors some typically clothed Parsee men and women. A bearded and turbaned taxi-driver, with a steel bracelet around his wrist is, he will be told, a Sikh.

He will pass many Hindus but not clearly recognize them as such until he encounters a man with three lines of sandal-wood paste drawn across his forehead—an orthodox Hindu, a devotee of Shiva, the god of destruction. On a street corner his attention may be arrested by a man in spotless white, with a mask like a surgeon's over his mouth. He is carefully brushing clean the path in front of him. This man is a Jain monk whose sincere religious intent is to do no harm to any living creature. At a railway station he may observe a saffron-robed monk with his head close-shaved. He is a Buddhist from Burma being met by some of the few adherents to that faith still living in the land of its founder. Occasionally at the same station he may be fortunate enough to see strange people with Mongolian features, not unlike American Indians in appearance. They might even be equipped with bows and arrows. They are perhaps Naga tribesmen, who practice primitive animism as do millions of their fellow countrymen.

Truly the people of India are very religious. In view of such diversity it is not strange that India has proclaimed herself a secular state. By this her leaders mean much the same that we do when we speak of separation of church and state. Her citizens are being slowly trained to regard themselves first of all as Indians and not primarily as members of one of the country's religious communities.

People are much less reticent in these lands about their religions than most Americans. Their rites are often practiced quite openly. It is therefore no great problem to discuss religion with almost anyone at any time. Leaders in the church, whether Indians or missionaries, do well to become as fully acquainted as possible with the principal religions of the country. It was Max Müller who said, "He who knows only his own religion knows none." It is difficult in considering other religions not to compare the best in our own faith with the worst in others. Current missionary technique does not involve an attempt to convince anyone by the comparison of religions. Comparisons are odious, particularly in such a context, though privately one can hardly fail to make them. We cannot regard lightly what others hold sacred.[1]

A Glimpse at Hinduism

Hinduism is the most important religion with which the church in India finds itself in contact. Hinduism really defies definition. It has been called "the inclusive term of the principal socio-religious trends of India." Again, a Hindu has been described as "a man who says he is one." Or the Hindus have been classified as all the Indians left after you subtract all Indians who profess allegiance to any other religion. It is not uncommon

---

[1] Note: In this connection it is mentioned that a Methodist missionary, the Rev. Arthur G. Atkins, has made a notable contribution to understanding. In 1953 he completed a translation in English verse of the much-loved Hindi poem, the *Ramayana,* by Tulsi Das, an Indian contemporary of Shakespeare. It is being published by the Hindustan *Times,* Delhi, managed by Gandhi's son, Devadas. This translation is being widely acclaimed by Indian scholars.

in America to hear all Indians mistakenly referred to as Hindus.

Sometimes there are said to be several Hinduisms. For example, there is a highly philosophical and metaphysical Hinduism, with which comparatively few Hindus themselves could be expected to be acquainted in detail. Another is sectarian Hinduism of which there are many, many varieties. Then there is popular Hinduism. As the term indicates, it is practiced by the masses of people in countless forms. It involves an endless variety of rites in the home and in the temple, though Hinduism knows no congregational worship as we understand it. It embraces pilgrimages, vast religious fairs, public shrines (a student has enumerated 1,400 in one city and is about half finished with his task), holy cities, holy rivers, holy animals, trees, and so on. Hinduism is an immense umbrella in the shade of which millions find comfort.

This religion has no historical founder nor sharply defined doctrine. An important sociological feature of the religion is the caste system. Every book that touches on the subject reminds the reader that there are four main castes: the priests and teachers; the ruler-warriors; the merchants and agriculturists; the servile group. Each is divided into numerous sub-castes, the whole totalling possibly three thousand. A fifth grouping, in reality outside the pale of Hinduism, is variously termed Outcastes, Untouchables, Depressed Classes, Scheduled Castes, or, by Gandhi, called *Harijans,* God's people. They number about 60,000,000 out of a total of about 300,000,000 Hindus.

Caste is of complex and multiple origin, explained in a variety of ways. Some counterpart to it for Greek life is described in Plato's *Republic.* This device of social organization is by no means the unmixed evil it is frequently considered. It has some positive values for society. It is nevertheless breaking down, though it shows a lot of vitality even yet. Its water-tight compartments forbidding intermarriage and inter-dining and restricting occupation are slowly yielding to the pressures and influences of modern times, of migration to cities, exposure to

Western ideas and Christianity as well as to the whole world-wide ferment among the "common men" in our century.

A visitor to India met a high caste schoolteacher. The latter said proudly, "See! Caste is breaking down. We Brahmins will now allow another to touch us. I will shake hands with you." The stranger was pleased and said, "Fine, will you also have dinner with me?" To which the teacher replied, "No, I haven't gone that far yet."

India's new constitution outlaws untouchability. An Indian was speaking of this achievement in New York. An American rather cynically asked him how long it would be before the outcaste enjoyed equal rights in actual fact and not just on the statute books. His reply was to ask in turn of his enquirer how long it would be before Negro Americans enjoyed equality in the United States, despite three constitutional amendments guaranteeing the same. It is a situation in which neither Americans nor Indians are in a position to throw stones.

Hinduism is pantheistic; that is, it insists that God is all, and all is God. It tends strongly toward the mystical, emphasizing oneness of man with deity. It conceives of one Ultimate Being, the impersonal deity, Brahman. All being is identical with this Supreme Being. The individual soul or *atman* is in fact one with the universal soul. "The *atman* is the universal Brahman in the breast." This intuitive idea is fundamental to Hinduism, and its basic search or aim is the realization of this identity. This is the secret of the *Upanishads*, the Hindu holy writings, and is endlessly explored and expounded in the massive sacred literature of Hinduism. The ways or paths toward this realization of oneness with the Eternal are three in number, suited to the capacity and disposition of a given individual: the way of works; the way of loving devotion; the way of knowledge. Only the latter brings final release.

There is a formula which describes the ends of conduct for the Hindu. It may be translated: Duty—Livelihood—Pleasure —Liberation. Every man has his religious *duty* of fulfilling the role that his caste position in society dictates. He engages in *work* necessary to support himself and his family in the ordinary affairs of life. He gives expression to the emotional and intellectual *pleasures* of life—the "joy of living." But finally he aims at the *liberation* or release (*moksha* or salvation) from the eternal round of rebirths by identification with the Supreme.

Of course, the average Hindu villager could not be expected to be very familiar with the above. Since Hinduism accommodates itself to many levels, the Universal God, remote and impersonal, would not be worshiped by such a person; but for him there are lesser deities represented by images or idols in temples.

Hinduism, far from decaying, is experiencing a revival in India today. It has been going on a long time. More than a hundred and twenty-five years ago there was established a famous reformed Hindu sect called the *Brahmo Samaj*. This is a small group, greatly influenced by Christianity. The poet, Rabindranath Tagore, was a member. Fifty years later was established the *Arya Samaj* with the purpose of reviving the pure and original Aryan Hinduism. This body is ardent and active in India today in its espousal of Hinduism and opposition to Christianity. A few years later the Ramakrishna Mission was established. It engages in much good social work in India, after the Christian missionary pattern, and in addition sends foreign missionaries abroad, a number to the United States. Here they have established Vedanta Societies promulgating the ideas of mystical identity. Other reform societies of similar purpose have been established in considerable numbers in various parts of India. In addition, this revival has been given political expression through a party called the Hindu Mahasabha which aims at the establishment of a Hindu India, replacing the secular state. A militant arm of this group, called the R.S.S., was responsible for the assassination of Mahatma Gandhi.

This revival has been a reaction to contact with the West. Hinduism has shown remarkable adaptability. In its contact with Western thought it has at various times retreated, remained aloof, been absorptive; now it is renascent, revived, undergoing reinterpretation and becoming aggressive.

Hinduism confronts the church with an emphasis on tolerance. In some respects this is commendable but at times such tolerance is insisted upon so vigorously as to be intolerant of those who are not like-minded.

Related to the above is the Hindu tendency to syncretism—to declare that all religions are the same and that there is nothing to choose between them. No concept is more insistent in India today. According to it, all faiths are roads leading to God. All roads lead to the top of the mountain, and it matters little which one you take. A Hindu student said, "If you want to go to the second floor of a building, it does not matter whether you take an elevator, climb the stairs or a ladder, or are drawn up by a rope."

At a recent exhibition in North India in one booth was a display of the Hindu deity, Krishna, with a picture of Gandhi in his heart. Behind that was the Cross. Behind that was Buddha. Hinduism gladly acknowledges Jesus Christ as a great religious teacher but is prepared to regard him as in no way unique.

The Christian Position

This doctrine, as stated, the Christian cannot accept. To him Christ is the central, unique fact of history before whom all men are called to decision. To proclaim this fact, in all humility, and still to relate itself to the stream of Indian culture and address itself to the needs of Indian people is the formidable task engaging the church there today. Recalling the figure of the paths up the mountain, the Christian might reply that Christ is a shepherd who makes his way down the mountain to help all men to the top. He might suggest to the student that there is only *one* way to the second floor of the building and that is to overcome the power of gravity! He declares that his essential faith is not simply another religion alongside the many already being professed in India. It is a gospel set forth in answer to the deep demands of all men. With St. Paul he humbly says, "We preach not ourselves but Christ."

In such religious surroundings, between Christian and non-Christian there is sometimes friction; sometimes resentment and discrimination, especially directed toward the minority group. There is also opportunity to witness. There is also interchange, both conscious and unconscious.

Some Christian Indians would hasten the process of bringing Christianity more fully into the stream of Indian culture. They recall that the gospel comes to them clothed in Western garments. Adolph Harnack said that Christian dogma "is the work of the Greek spirit on the soil of the gospel." This process of Indianization is difficult and can be perilous. But it is also necessary, if the Christian faith is to survive on Indian soil. A new Christian apologetic is overdue in India and Pakistan today and must be cast in terms which the intelligent Hindu and Muslim will understand. A Christian institution, the Henry Martyn School of Islamics, is helpful in this regard; and there is a current effort to establish centers for the careful Christian study of other religious and cultural backgrounds in India.

Since this process must, if it is to have value and validity, take place in India, it is perhaps idle to suggest what line the development may pursue. The essential gospel must be distinguished from its Western trappings. Fundamentally, that Jesus is God Incarnate, the fact that He entered history, and the fact of His redemptive work must all be asserted. The uniqueness of Jesus and his work are basic. Can these be expressed in terms not alien to India? Is it possible to express them *through* Indian cultural means, without identifying the Christian message with Indian culture?

To some Christians this is regarded as an impossible task, for in their thinking there is no meeting between the gospel and non-Christian faiths. Other Christians, however, find in the great religions a soil prepared for the gospel. All religions are a reaching for God. The gospel is God's response, revealing Himself to men through Jesus Christ. In the thinking of some Christians the endeavor, therefore, must be not to destroy but to fulfill. The Indian religious heritage, for example, affords a veritable mine in the form of religious vocabulary which, redefined, has served the church well. This process can continue.

The Indian emphasis on religion related to all life is of value. The Indian capacity for sacrifice, renunciation, and loving devotion; the regard for peace, self-control, simplicity; the longing for fulfillment—all are certainly of value. So, too, the emphasis on the individual expressing himself through the group, though often overdone in Hinduism, is worth while. Some traditional techniques, such as religious fairs, ashrams, art forms, music, have already served the gospel well and will undoubtedly do so in the future.

An Indian, later a bishop, has written:

"Like some immense cathedral, Christianity will rise in India with that majesty and dignity which are especially its own. Whatever we take over from Hinduism will be to Christianity what the buttresses are to a cathedral. These buttresses do not constitute the building by any means. The vast spaces of the cathedral, the stained-glass windows through which the light streams in wonderful loveliness, the lofty roof with its finely wrought ceiling, the ornate pillars with their majestic proportions, the altar and chancel in their glory—these do not depend upon their buttresses for their beauty of grace. And yet the buttresses add considerably to the stability and strength of the mighty structure. To confuse the main structure with the buttresses would be as great a mistake as to confuse Christianity with the elements which it may absorb from Hinduism. The religion of Christ is unique." [2]

Now Glance at Islam

Though Islam is by no means a negligible factor in India today, we turn to Pakistan. The church there finds itself in an

---

[2] *What is Moksa?* A. J. Appasamy, Madras: Christian Literature Society, 1931, p. 16.

Islamic state and amid Muslim culture. Thus far the country
has been ruled by Muslims of liberal persuasion. There are also
quite vocal orthodox Muslims who challenge the liberal view-
point. Religious liberty has been a fact, in sharp contrast to
what obtains in some Mohammedan lands. A number of Muslims in Pakistan have been converted to the Christian faith
since Independence. It is well to remember, though, that during
the last 1,300 years more Christians have become Muslims than
the other way around.

Pakistan is at present engaged in framing its constitution.
There is promise that religious freedom will be provided for in it.
An effort will be made to see that as the constitution of an
Islamic state it contains no law repugnant to the Koran. The
church may have soon to decide whether or not it will teach
about Islam in Christian schools.

It is no less important for Christians in Pakistan to understand Islam than it is for them to have an understanding of
Hinduism in India. Islam means "submitted," and a Muslim
is one who is submitted to God. Muslims are called "people of
the book" because of their sacred Koran. They call both Christians and Jews "people of the book" too, thus acknowledging a
kind of kinship with these two groups. Islam has no priesthood
but does have various types of religious teachers and specialists
in the law. Though theoretically Muslims have no caste, the
Hindu influence has been such that in Southern Asia there are
clear class distinctions among them. There are also many sects.
Like Christianity, but unlike Hinduism, Islam stems from an
historical founder, Mohammed. They have not built temples
but mosques. Such buildings have left a deep stamp on Indian
architecture. Though not a mosque but a tomb, the Taj Mahal
at Agra is the greatest example of Muslim architecture. In
its geometric loveliness it has been called a "symphony in
stone."

As an elementary description of Muslim faith and practice
it is suggested that Islam has six basic beliefs: (1) *Belief in*

Allah. Islam is radical monotheism. (2) *Angels.* These include Gabriel and many others the average Christian has not heard of. A good Muslim will not whistle, for example, for by that means the angels communicate with one another. (3) *Books.* As already indicated, they recognize the Jewish Law, the Psalms, and the Gospels, as well as their own Koran. Some Muslims learn the whole Koran by heart. (4) *Prophets.* They recognize Jesus as a prophet, as well as Abraham, Moses, and some others. But to the Muslim, Mohammed is the greatest, the last or "seal" of the prophets. (5) *Judgment.* At the last day there will be a reckoning before Allah. (6) *Decrees of good and evil.* This is predestination; Allah decrees and determines at birth all men's lives whether for good or evil.

The basic practical duties for good Muslims are five in number, called the "Five Pillars of Islam"; (1) *The confession*— "There is no god but Allah and Mohammed is his prophet." This is whispered to a child in many Muslim homes even before he can talk. (2) *The ritual prayers.* These are at five stated times each day, to be performed according to careful routine. (3) *Fasting.* There are a number of fasts prescribed but particularly the abstinence from all food and drink during daylight hours throughout one particular month each year— Ramadan or Ramzan. (4) *Almsgiving.* Usually a prescribed amount, say, a twentieth of one's income is to be given to the needy. (5) *The Pilgrimage.* Every good Muslim is supposed to go to the holy city of Mecca once during his lifetime. Of course, most cannot do this.

This skeletal analysis of Islam does far less than justice to it. Like Hinduism, it is a culture, a whole way of life with ramifications into every aspect of living. This very fact accounts for the deep severance when one becomes a Christian from such a background. Once again, it gives point to the necessity for Christianity not to be presented in garments which are too foreign.

Islam is sometimes called a "Christian heresy." It does **have** the unique position of being a religion which developed subsequent to Christianity and has often been in conflict with it. Furthermore, in some parts of the world Islam has virtually supplanted Christianity. Since there is something of a kinship between the Judeo-Christian and the Muslim heritage, it is becoming more possible to explain the Christian understanding of various matters to Muslims. The atmosphere seems to be improving in this respect nowadays and perhaps in few places so much as in Pakistan. Surely the church must avail itself of these new opportunities.

In both India and Pakistan an increasing measure of secularism and materialism is evident. For example, many educated Muslims do not nowadays pay much heed to the beliefs and practices mentioned above. This secular development distresses Muslim and Hindu religious leaders as much as it does Christian leaders in other parts of the world. To the degree that this development takes place, the gospel can be presented to the secular-minded in these countries on much the same terms it is presented to the secular-minded in other parts of the world.

To conclude this section a pertinent incident is recounted. Sometime ago a Hindu gentleman was asked by a young people's group in India to talk about his religion. He began, strangely enough, by reading aloud the Sermon on the Mount. He then gave a highly idealized picture of Hinduism. His listeners objected: "But we don't know any Hindus who live like that." His reply was that that was why he began by reading the Sermon on the Mount. He did not know any Christians who lived like that!

About Missionaries

Something has been said about the political, cultural, and religious setting in which the church finds itself in Southern Asia today. The principal burden of the task is rightfully borne there by Christian Indians at the present time. If circumstances should arise in India and Pakistan such as have arisen in some other

parts of the world, and missionaries could no longer serve
there, the church could carry on in spite of this handicap. In
some parts of the countries, however, the church would suffer
or even disappear. Happily such a situation has not arisen.

Missionaries have in the past played an immensely important
role in this part of the world. A history of the 19th century in
India would be incomplete without giving wide attention to
their contribution. One viceroy, Lord Lawrence, admitted that
missionaries had done more to benefit the country "than all other
agencies combined." It is important to view the missionary in
his present context.

Are Missionaries Needed?

Such a question cannot adequately be answered by an out-
sider. Within India there is a divided opinion about the matter expressed by non-Christians. Militant Hindu or Muslim
groups would answer decisively, "No!" Some, reflecting a
strong nationalist position, would say that the presence of
foreigners is an unhappy reminder of an earlier period of
colonial domination. More moderate opinion would be that in
the difficult process of building newly free nations, as many
trained persons of goodwill as possible are needed and welcome.

It is within the church, however, that a fuller answer is to
be looked for. Even there, a minority would say that the day
of the foreign missionary is over. Sometimes this is a sincere
conviction; sometimes it reflects a justifiable feeling of resentment over unhappy personal relations with a missionary; sometimes it indicates personal ambition. On the whole, however,
the church welcomes the missionary though it wishes to qualify
his role.

One expression of this point of view appears in a recent book
by a Christian Indian layman:

"There is natural antipathy to anything that seems foreign controlled.
This does not, however, mean that we shall no longer need the as-

sistance of the older Churches in personnel, funds and counsel. The
Church of India will, for a long time to come, continue to need these
and will be prepared to welcome as colleagues brethren in the faith from
older Churches. . . . India will need missionaries from the West, it
would appear, for all time and for a long time will need financial
help. Let that be frankly stated. . . .

". . . At the present time, when India is standing at the crossroads
of her destiny and is in sore need of men of character, and with the
Christian striking force so small, so economically handicapped and so
meagerly equipped, mentally and spiritually, the Church and the Christian community in India need to be strengthened by all the support
which the older churches of the West can give. Christian charity
demands it. Christian policy requires it. There is the need, and there
will always be a welcome, in India for the consecrated man and woman
who, impelled by the love of God in Jesus Christ, respond to the
imperatives of the Gospel and come out 'to minister and not to be
ministered to.' " [8]

Another prominent layman says: "Send us good men and
women; we don't care so much for money as for men." They
urge at the same time that they should not come to lead but
to serve as equal partners; they must "enjoy the background."
Every missionary in relationship to his colleagues of the country
in which he serves needs to learn the lesson of John the Baptist;
"He must increase, but I must decrease." This is a difficult
lesson.

Though the majority of Christian Indians would say that
missionaries are needed, they would go on to describe the *kind*
of missionary they have in mind. They are interested in their
attitudes, and in their having deep and pure motives. How ex-
acting the missionary role is will be seen in this list handed
to the writer by a well-known Indian, describing missionary
qualities:

"(1) Above all he should be Christ-intoxicated; to him Christ should
be all in all. (2) He should come not only as a teacher but also as a

[8] *The Cross Over India,* by Rajaiah D. Paul, London: S.C.M. Press Ltd.,
(1952) pp. 122-124.

learner. (3) He should come in a spirit of brotherhood and fellowship and with no sense of pity wrapped in superiority. (4) He should come not as a destroyer but as a fulfiller of that which is best in India's culture and spiritual quest. (5) His training should be of a high order in the sphere in which he is to serve, and part of his training should be undertaken in the land of his adoption. (6) He should not be a denominationalist but an ardent lover of church union. (7) Evangelization of India should be his passion. (8) He should wholeheartedly identify himself with the church on the field. (9) He should come as an utter believer in India's political freedom, with no sign of imperialism in his makeup. (10) The spirit of patience and humility should be one of his chief adornments in the midst of so much that will be irksome, distasteful, and foreign. (11) The advancing of Indian leadership should be one of his main concerns, so that ultimately he himself may become unnecessary. (12) All co-operative efforts should have the right of way with him."

The missionary is still needed principally for these reasons:
(1) His presence is needed to give spiritual tone to the church. From the outside he can show greater objectivity. He need not be swayed unduly by the ofttimes petty considerations which enter into the daily life of the church.

(2) Of more basic importance, he is needed to share in the unfinished task of the church: "that they might know thee the only true God, and Jesus Christ whom thou hast sent."

(3) The missionary is needed as a constant reminder of the supranational character of the church. It is not merely national or regional, but universal. This note is needed throughout the world and argues for mutual interchange of Christian personnel. How greatly the church in America benefits nowadays by the more frequent association with Christian visitors from overseas!

Are Missionaries Still Wanted?

On this related question, opinion is also divided both inside and outside the church in Southern Asia. A missionary is not prompted to serve primarily because he is wanted or appreciated. If that were the criterion, the Christian faith would not have spread outside Palestine and indeed would have perished there. Rather, the missionary incentive is prompted by obedience to a deep sense of the will of God, especially in response to the commission Jesus has given His Church to go and "make disciples of all the nations." One scholar of missions has written: "True mission work never depends on results, which may encourage or depress us, but only on belief in our Lord who sends His messengers into the world."[4]

Missionaries *are* appreciated for the most part. Mrs. Vijaya-lakshmi Pandit, sister of Prime Minister Nehru, said in New York:

"I should like to take this opportunity to express the gratitude of many sections of my people for the splendid contributions that foreign missionaries have made to India in promoting the welfare of its people. Mission hospitals, schools, colleges, asylums, welfare settlements, and rural development centers that have been established in different parts of India by voluntary effort of the foreign missionaries have always been both an inspiration and an example. In the secular state of India, we hope to welcome many friends of foreign missions in the task of the great construction on which we have launched."

At the other end of the social scale a village Christian addressed missionaries with gratitude: "Before you came, we were as little children; now we are growing up. Before you came, we were oppressed and poor and wasteful; now things are very much better."

Nevertheless the presence of the missionary is currently being challenged to a degree which is without precedent in modern India. This is in contrast to the fact that at the same time the missionary in Pakistan is comparatively unfettered. There is greater delay and difficulty than formerly in securing visas for missionaries to enter India for service, especially for direct evangelism. This is not to suggest that India is aflame with

---

[4] *Spiritual Revolution in the East,* by Walter Freytag, Lutterworth Press, London (1940), page 3.

universal animosity toward Christian missionaries. As indicated, appreciation of their work is often expressed. The majority of the people undoubtedly favor their presence. Mr. Nehru has repeatedly stated that "Christianity is as much the religion of India as any other religion. It has been here for the last nineteen hundred years." Various militant Hindu groups, which have already been mentioned, are quite vocal and influential in their anti-missionary attitudes.

During the first eight years of independence, the official attitude toward missionaries has been unobjectionable. It is said that in 1954 there were more missionaries in India than ever before. Religious freedom was guaranteed in the Indian Constitution as follows: "Subject to public order . . . all persons are equally entitled to . . . the right freely to profess, practice, and propagate religion." Indians have not only established this right for themselves; they must continuously uphold it. Officially, the Government of India declared during 1954 that its policy regarding entrance of missionaries had not changed. In practice, they are being more carefully screened than ever before, and some are being denied entrance.

Why should this be? From among many complex factors four are mentioned:

First, it is an outgrowth of *nationalism*. The presence of foreigners—whether missionaries or others—touches the feeling of pride and self-sufficiency very deeply. This is felt in some degree within the church as well as outside it. In itself this is not vastly different from other countries. It is hard for foreigners to enter the United States. So in India there is an increasing suspicion of foreigners, particularly in border areas.

Secondly, and more important, it is an expression of *religious nationalism*, for in Asia nationalism often takes a religious turn. A country which has received much from the West has a tendency to want to preserve its "soul"—its religious heritage —intact. Thus for extremists India is the "land of the Hindus."

Among Hindus there exists a suspicion of conversion. They do not distinguish it from proselytization, which we would think of as offering material inducements to conversion. A government official recently asked a missionary, "Can't you carry on your work without converting people?" The reply was: "It is not I who convert people to Christ but the Holy Spirit working in their hearts. Who would disrespect the work of God?" Did the official understand? Gandhi said, "If a man has a living faith in him, it spreads its aroma like the rose its scent." There is some truth here, and much Christian effort in India does just that; but there comes a time when an explanation must be given as to why a Christian serves people.

Thirdly, there are *internal political factors* which prompt anti-missionary attitudes. Hindus have seen their country split by Muslims who agitated for the separate nation of Pakistan. They say they fear a repetition of this from other minority groups. When a Hindu becomes a Christian, it is one less Hindu vote.

Finally, there are *external political factors*. Some Indians do not wish to believe that missionaries are not related to their homeland governments. For example, when the United States gives military aid to Pakistan, American missionaries are suspect.

Quite apart from missionaries, the church itself in India does not escape being the target of hostile attitudes. This experience is not entirely unhealthy for the church. Christians have repeatedly risen to defend their own rights and have spoken in behalf of their missionary colleagues. As nearly always is the case, a certain amount of pressure has a purifying effect upon the church. If anything, it has driven Christians to a more wholehearted devotion to Christ. These events are encouraging a growth in self-reliance as well as reliance upon God.

In one part of India the state government is investigating conversions in the villages. Village Christians are saying such things as this: "See, we must be important people. They are coming to investigate us. They want to know what we believe. Maybe our Christian religion is important in India. Why else would the Hindu government officials come to us if they were not afraid of the power of our religion?" Christians in an Indian non-Christian society have never been entirely free from a measure of persecution and pressure. But fair-minded non-Christians often speak out strongly in defense of Christians and missionaries.

It is possible that there will be a gradual reduction of missionaries in India over a period of time. This is not contradictory with what was contemplated from the very beginning of the enterprise there. Fortunately, God has all along been raising up able Indian leaders to engage in the task.

In the midst of such circumstances missionaries are not panicky, nor are they indulging in complaint. The churches in India and the National Christian Council there are registering their attitudes with their government. If Christians have to undergo difficulties and hardships, then they rediscover that to be a Christian is not necessarily to be safe and comfortable but that it may involve sharing deeply the suffering and rejection of the Lord.

In Article 19 of the Universal Declaration of Human Rights we read:

"Everyone has the right to freedom of opinion and expression; the right includes freedom to hold opinions without interference and to seek, receive and impart information and ideas through any media and regardless of frontiers."

Of course, this has not yet been adopted as a covenant by the United Nations. If and until that time comes, missionaries will continue to work where it is possible for them to work. They are grateful that they can work with their friends in Pakistan and India.

Missionaries Are Adjusting

A missionary is "one who is sent." In Dutch there is a more expressive word for missionary than in English; it is *sendling*. With St. Augustine he says, "What I live by, that I impart."

Dr. John R. Mott called the missionary "the true internationalist." Others theorize on the subject; he acts on it. As he goes out he finds he represents more than he had anticipated. He finds he is not only a missionary, but the representative of the West and its culture too. He often has to rid himself of excess baggage so that he can be as fundamentally Christian as possible.

In the West, if a missionary is not thought of with scorn, folk tend to indulge in heroics about him. He does not feel heroic; he does not desire admiration and, above all, does not want pity. Even when it is perplexing, the average missionary loves his work because he loves people. If he does not, he does not continue. One writes, "During the years we have made friends of some of the world's choicest people." Regarding their work, missionaries say: "My church makes it *possible* for me to do what I am convinced God *wants* me to do." "To think that I might have missed being a missionary!"

Yet it is not easy. It is a strain to live in another culture; to express oneself in another language. Life at home in familiar surroundings has many reinforcements. When these are removed, the roots must go deep into the things which cannot be shaken.

It is not easy to work amid times of change; still they are adjusting. A missionary engineer from India writes: "We are standing in the period of transition where we see so much of the old and of the new. There is no time like the present to be in India, working to help her stand on her two feet with self-respect among the nations of the world. And we as engineers have a real place here. . ."

Many complain that the missionary lives on too high a standard—too far removed from the average Indian. Some are experimenting with simpler living. One family lived modestly in an Indian village for a while. Naturally the villagers were curious, and one day they counted twenty faces at a screened window. They laughed at the experience, saying, "We don't believe we will ever again have the heart to go to the zoo and watch the monkeys in the cage." Another lived in rented quarters in a crowded urban area occupied by Christian families. Another took seriously the missionary instructions Jesus gave his disciples. "Take nothing for your journey, neither staff, nor wallet, nor bread, nor money; neither have two coats." Leaving his jeep behind and starting out with the clothes on his back and a New Testament, he walked among the villages. They fed him and gave him shelter. About the experience he said, "Never did I have such a reception!"

Missionaries are adjusting to giving their witness even under difficult and sometimes hostile circumstances. If formal methods of presentation of the Christian message are sometimes hampered, the life itself often becomes the message. For example, a lady missionary on a train one day fell into conversation with an educated Hindu. After some time he inquired why she had come to India. She said: "Christ called me to India and I try to serve Him here as my Saviour and Lord." He replied: "You're full of Him, aren't you?" Gandhi constantly encouraged missionaries to let their lives speak for Jesus Christ. When the life speaks, then occasions constantly arise in both India and Pakistan today when the reason for one's faith can also be shared.

Missionaries are adjusting to serving under the direction of their Indian friends. One who recently retired said with approval: "Forty years ago at annual conference we missionaries did all the talking, and the Indians remained silent. Now they do all the talking, and we remain silent. That's progress." It is a sign of maturity too that on most questions some Indians and some missionaries vote on each side in deliberative bodies.

Another missionary rode in a third-class compartment on the train. He talked with some fellow ministers of the matters touched on in this chapter. Finally, he said to them: "Some of you men are going to make *church* history in India; not just *mission* history." They made no reply, but after a moment the whole group broke into the Gujarati version of Charles Wesley's hymn, "O for a thousand tongues to sing my great Redeemer's praise."

CHAPTER IV

INDIAN METHODIST BEGINNINGS

DURING THE early 1850's two British engineers— brothers they were—were building a railway across the Great Indian Desert. One started from Karachi and the other from Lahore—a kind of Indian variety of Union Pacific. For lack of stone they often encountered difficulty in securing ballast for the track bed. Then one of them found ancient mounds over long-buried cities. He carted away the debris from them for ballast. When this word was shared with the other brother, he did likewise from other sites. Actually it was a kind of archeological crime, for decades later it was discovered that these ruins were among the world's most ancient cities. How great was the loss no one will ever know. Thus, as one rides today by rail between these two cities in comparative comfort, he is moving over a lot of past history!

Likewise, one moves over much Christian history in Southern Asia. It is well to examine it a bit.

It may seem surprising that many of the first Methodist missionaries to India were sent out on ice! This is fact, not fancy. Many of the Yankee clippers to Calcutta, round the Cape of Good Hope, carried ice from New England ponds—ice to cool the drinks of overheated British civil servants. Also, the cargo often included apples—and missionaries!

Christian Foundations in India

Actually the story must go back further. Tradition assigns to Christianity in India apostolic origin. It can neither be proved nor disproved that the doubting apostle, St. Thomas, evangelized India. In 1952 was widely celebrated the nineteen hundredth anniversary of his supposed arrival there, which was about the time of St. Paul's arrival in Europe. Thomas is supposed to have met a martyr's death near St. Thomas Mount in the vicinity of Madras.

In any case there is a persistent "Thomas tradition" in South India. Various bits of evidence associate Christianity with the peninsula during the early centuries of our era. These traditions continue until today in the several churches of Syrian rite in Malabar on the southwest Indian coast. Prior to Roman Catholic influence, these churches were entirely separate from Rome. A part of these people have now, however, acknowledged papal allegiance.

One of the most interesting of these churches is the Mar Thoma Syrian church. Something over a hundred years ago it underwent a revival and reformation. This was under the leadership of Abraham Malpan, called "the Martin Luther of Travancore." The church is now warmly evangelical. Something of its spirit may be seen in the testimony of their late Metropolitan, Bishop Abraham. He once said that although his church had 200,000 members, he would be willing to see it vanish away if the reign of Christ could go forward in India. In explanation he told of viewing from his mountain home one summer dozens of villages in the plains below. These were but a few of the 600,000 villages of India. It suddenly occurred to him that he would be willing to see his people scatter over the face of India, going two by two to 100,000 of these villages. This would mean that his church would cease to be in the sense in which he had known it, but it would also mean the advance of the kingdom. In effect, he was saying that he was prepared for his church to do a very Christlike thing, to lose itself in order to find itself in a greater way. There is a genuineness about such a conviction!

Roman Catholic Beginnings

Vasco da Gama reached India in 1498. Soon afterward papal decree divided the newly discovered world between Portugal and Spain. India fell to the former. It is interesting that in justification of her claim today to tiny bits of Indian territory, such as Goa, Portugal cites a papal bull of the 15th century!

With the navigators came priests. A few years later they were successful in baptizing fishermen castes on the southeast coast of India.

The most successful early Catholic missionary was the Jesuit, St. Francis Xavier. He arrived in India in 1542. His contact in India was somewhat superficial, but his work met with phenomenal success. In the ten years before his death in 1552 he worked also in the East Indies, China, and Japan. He knew no Indian language and spent less than five years there. Thousands were nevertheless baptized, and he is greatly revered even today, especially in Goa.

Another Catholic missionary of note, also a Jesuit, was Robert de Nobili. He served in India from 1605 until his death in 1656. In contrast to his predecessors who had labored among Indians of humble background, he aimed by almost fantastic means at the conversion of Brahmins. He and his colleagues adopted the manner of living and dress of this group, became vegetarians, and announced themselves to be "European Brahmins." This involved a complete mastery of Hinduism. They claimed the discovery of a "lost sacred book" of Hinduism, a translation of parts of the Gospels. Though these extreme methods met with only moderate success, the mission historian, Julius Richter, calls him "one of the great missionaries of India."

Nevertheless Roman Catholicism has grown, and as already indicated there are as many Catholics as Protestants in India. Their educational facilities are about equal in size to those of Protestants, though the latter have until recently done much more in medical service. The Catholics are nowadays rapidly Indianizing their leadership. One cardinal and a number of bishops are Indian citizens. Moreover, India exchanges diplomatic representation with the Vatican City.

Protestant Beginnings

We tend to forget that the leaders of the Protestant Reformation were not missionary minded. They thought more in terms of national churches and, besides, their hands must have been full in other ways. Missionary endeavor was aroused much later.

The first Protestant missionaries to India were Bartholomew Ziegenbalg and Henry Plütschau. Germans, they were sent by King Frederick IV of Denmark to a small Danish settlement south of Madras, Tranquebar, where they arrived in 1706. Though they encountered many difficulties, especially from skeptical Europeans posted there, nevertheless Ziegenbalg especially made a notable record. He translated much of the Bible into Tamil.

Skipping over much of interest, we come to the real pioneer of modern missions, William Carey, who arrived in India in 1793. Encountering obstacles at Calcutta he settled in Serampore, a Danish colony north of the city, in 1800. There he was joined by his colleagues, Joshua Marshman and William Ward. They became known as "the Serampore trio."

So striking was the Serampore Covenant framed in 1805 by these three men, that it is given here:

"To set an infinite value on the individual soul.
To esteem and treat Indians always as our equals.
To abstain from whatever deepens India's prejudice.
To engage in every work that is for India's good.
To be instant in the nurture of personal religion.
To give ourselves without reserve, not counting even the clothes we wear our own."

Though a cobbler in early life, Carey was an intellectual giant. He, with his co-workers, translated the whole of the Bible into six languages, the whole New Testament into twenty-three, portions of the Bible into ten. This record is in striking contrast to the Catholics, who, although they first arrived more than two hundred years before the Protestants, made not one complete translation of the Scriptures. Largely supporting himself and his mission, Carey pioneered in nearly every other type of missionary endeavor that has since been undertaken. Furthermore, he started the seminary at Serampore which today is the sole degree-granting institution for all seminaries in India.

One more Protestant pioneer must be mentioned. He is the famous Scots educational missionary, Dr. Alexander Duff. Shipwrecked twice on the way to India, he arrived in Calcutta in 1830, a youth in his twenties. Almost immediately he launched out in a vast effort to train and capture the minds of non-Christian boys through the medium of English instruction. He aimed through access to the children of the higher classes to spread Christian knowledge through this group and so equip the church with highly talented leaders. During the early years particularly he was quite successful in furthering this purpose.

It was Alexander Duff who came to New York in 1854 and helped to stimulate the Methodist Missionary Society to enter the India field. He was made an "honorary member" of the society at that time.

Other principal boards in the United States, such as the Presbyterian and Congregationalist, had already been working in India for a number of years. When the first American Methodists arrived, however, there were hardly more than 100,000 Protestants in the whole Indian empire.

"The Father and Mother of the Mission"

Methodists were slow starters in foreign missions, largely because their energies went at first to rapid expansion in America. Beginning in 1852 the Missionary Society of the Methodist Episcopal Church set aside a sum of $7,500 to launch the Indian mission. This was renewed year by year until 1856 when the then secretary, Dr. John P. Durbin, finally found a volunteer to undertake leadership of the Indian work. It was said that no prominent post in the church was "ever declined by so many nominees."

The task was finally accepted by William Butler, a preacher of the New England Conference. Born in Ireland in 1818, he had come to the United States in 1850. Butler was a pioneer indeed, for later he founded the work of the Methodist Episcopal Church in Mexico in 1873. Dr. Butler had waited for others to accept the invitation to India; but since no one came forward, he offered himself. He was given wide discretionary power by Dr. Durbin both in his work and the selection of a location. Bishop Matthew Simpson advised him to "lay broad and deep foundations in India." [1]

The Butlers sailed immediately for India, arriving in Calcutta on September 25, 1856. They transshipped by land from Cairo to Suez, since the canal was not open until 1870. From Calcutta one could travel toward North Central India about a hundred miles by rail. From that point, Butler bought a wagon which was drawn by coolies for several hundred miles. He chose as his field one which was entirely unoccupied at the time by other missionaries. It covered much of what is now Uttar Pradesh or United Provinces. He desired to start work at Lucknow, but no housing was available. They proceeded to Bareilly, reaching this birthplace of Indian Methodism in December, 1856. On the way, Butler had secured as a helper a preacher from the Presbyterians in Allahabad, Joel Janvier, the first Indian Methodist preacher. The first Methodist services in English and Hindustani were held on Sunday, February 25, 1857.

Hardly had work begun before the Mutiny broke out in May of that year. With the insurgents at the doors Janvier was preaching on the text: "Fear not, little flock, for it is the Father's good pleasure to give you the kingdom." Since then it has been a symbol and rallying cry of Indian Methodism. All escaped except one, and a few minutes later the mutineers

---

[1] *William Butler,* Clementina Butler, New York: Eaton and Mains, 1902, p. 38.

had beheaded the first Anglo-Indian adherent, Maria Bolst, the first martyr also, of our church in India. The Butlers a few days earlier had barely escaped with their lives to the mountains at Naini Tal, where they remained for months. All other missionaries in that part of India were killed. Butler too was assumed to be dead, and Duff wrote his obituary!

Meanwhile two other families had sailed and were finally met by Butler in Agra, where the party sang the Doxology under the dome of the Taj Mahal. Work could not be started again until late in 1858. The next year, the missionary group was further reinforced by a party including James M. Thoburn and Edwin W. Parker, both of whom later became bishops of the church.

William Butler did not himself gain mastery of the language but laid plans and cared for business details so that the others would be free for the actual work of evangelism. In fact, the success of the early mission was due not only to Butler but in large measure to the remarkable caliber of his colleagues. The Superintendent served only temporarily, returning ill to the homeland in 1865. The Butlers revisited their field for a triumphal tour in 1883 and Mrs. Butler came again for the Golden Jubilee in 1906. Their daughter was present for the Diamond Jubilee in 1931.

The first convert responded to the preaching of the Reverend J. L. Humphreys. He was a Muslim named Zahur-ul-Haqq. He later became a preacher and in 1882 the first Indian district superintendent.

Now for a few more firsts. The first church was dedicated in Naini Tal in October, 1858. The first institution was an orphanage, founded the same year in Lucknow for children whose parents were killed in the Mutiny. Of the original group of 150 girls, 87 of them were twenty-five years later in Christian work. A printing press was started in 1861. Humphreys studied medicine during his first furlough and upon return to the field started in 1867 training Indian girls to assist him. An industrial school was launched in 1868. Bareilly Seminary was started in 1870. The church paper, *The Indian Witness,* appeared the following year. Almost immediately all manner of activity was undertaken. The missionary statesman, Thoburn, was later to say: "The best missionary policy is that which avails itself of every agency out of which anything good can be wrought." [2]

The story is told by William Butler of attending Christmas service in 1857 in the great audience chamber—Dewan-i-khas —of the last Moghal Emperor. During that visit, he sat on the recently vacated throne and wrote letters to friends in America for orphanages and schools.

The India Mission Conference was established in 1864. This later became the North India Conference.

Work Among Women

Two notable events for Indian Methodism occurred in 1870. That year marked the arrival in the country of the first missionaries of the Woman's Foreign Missionary Society. They were Miss Isabella Thoburn, later to found the first college for women in all Asia, and Dr. Clara A. Swain, first woman medical missionary of any society and founder of the first hospital for women in Asia. They were the forerunners of hundreds of other single women who have since gone all over the world for Christian work, especially among women and children. It should not, of course, be forgotten that the wives of the earliest pioneer missionaries worked unstintingly with their husbands. To this day, both husbands and wives are commissioned, both are full-fledged missionaries, both engage in service. The whole church is indebted to the splendid work of the missionary wives whose Christian homes have in themselves constituted a monumental Christian witness.

It was fitting that these first women missionaries should

---

[2] *India and Malaysia,* James M. Thoburn, New York: Hunt and Eaton, 1892, p. 331.

have gone to India, for two ladies from India were influential in starting the Woman's Foreign Missionary Society. Mrs. William Butler and Mrs. Edwin W. Parker, who was on furlough from India with her husband at the time, mentioned to Mrs. Lewis Flanders in Boston the importance of a missionary society for women similar to one already in existence in the Congregational Church. Immediately the latter invited the other two to address a Ladies' Aid Society at Tremont Street Church. The next day, March 23, 1869, the Woman's Foreign Missionary Society was founded in that church. It was a rainy day, and only eight women were present. It was a day of small beginnings, but the society rapidly grew in size and effectiveness. Today, in union with its counterparts in the branches of Methodism which became one in 1939, it has grown to be the largest organization for women in the world!

A remarkable characteristic throughout the whole missionary enterprise during the last half of the nineteenth century was the rapid growth of work among women. Many handicaps and prejudices had to be overcome. The great Duff worked solely for education among young men. His oft-quoted remark was that "you might as well attempt to lift the loftiest peak in the Himalayas and throw it into the Bay of Bengal" as attempt the education of Indian girls. The many restraints placed upon women in Indian society lent some substance to this remark. It remained for Isabella Thoburn, among many others, to disprove it.

Early efforts among girls were through the medium of orphanages. Later on, day schools in the bazaars were founded. In Bareilly some of these latter were called "pice" schools, due to the fact that a "pice" (worth half a cent) was given to the girls for attending. Meanwhile, as many young men enjoyed the benefits of Western education, they began to insist that the girls who were to become their wives have some education.

Another missionary method was for women missionaries to

make their way into the *zenanas,* living quarters for Indian women, largely withdrawn from outside society. This custom, almost universal in North India where the influence of Muslim practices was strong, affected the manner of living of a third of all women in India. Likewise the ladies travelled to the villages, accompanied by Indian Bible women, in itinerant evangelism. Thus by education, by medicine, by social service, by evangelism did the women work among women and children in many parts of the country.

In reporting to the General Conference in 1892, Bishop Thoburn said: "Perhaps I might be pardoned if I venture to say that nowhere in Methodism, if indeed anywhere else in Christendom, is woman's work so fully recognized and so thoroughly organized as in the Methodist Episcopal Church in India." [3]

The Work of William Taylor

If the coming of the first women missionaries in 1870 broadened the social range of Indian Methodism, the other notable event of that same year, the coming of William Taylor to India, was responsible for broadening the geographical range. It was at the invitation of James M. Thoburn and a Baptist missionary that the great evangelist came to Southern Asia.

Taylor was one of the most effective evangelists of his century. His career was fabulous. Born in Virginia in 1820, he early entered the ministry. First of all, he was a home missionary to California, where he went in 1849. To the rough goldminers he was known as "Father Taylor" and later throughout the world as "California" Taylor. His missions took him all over the United States and Canada, to Britain, to Australia, to South Africa, to Ceylon, and to India, where he spent four years. He left India suddenly to join the great Moody and Sankey meetings in England. Later on he established a line of work around the coast of South America. Finally, he was elected in 1884

---

[3] Thoburn, *ibid.,* p. 541.

as bishop of Africa and spent a decade or more in the heart of that continent.

Taylor thus had an important part in the development of many of the present-day mission fields of our church. Though not always were his policies sound, at least he did not hesitate to think and act in strategic terms. The keystone of his policy was self-support, of which he gave personal demonstration. For years he maintained himself solely from the sale of his books. He felt that it was the method of St. Paul, the tentmaker. He promoted this idea in three continents—Southern Asia, Latin America, and Africa. It was his conviction that in the first two areas especially there were resources in the country for the support of missionaries. Under the power of his personality, when immediately present, this scheme was fairly successful. Later the Board of Missions had to take care of the support of many, though not all, of his missionaries who at one time had been supported locally.

Taylor began his work in the territory in north India which William Butler had chosen as a Methodist field. In this area he was only moderately successful, though he did revive the church considerably. The conviction grew on him that Methodism had as much right and reason to bear its witness throughout the whole country as did any other denomination, such as the Anglicans or Roman Catholics. This, of course, in the thinking of some people was to fly in the face of any recognition of comity, by which each group agreed to function only in certain areas. There was fierce debate against this position by those Methodists who felt the work would be more effective if concentrated in a smaller territory. In his views Taylor had a powerful ally in Thoburn, who, indeed, joined him in his extension program.

As has been mentioned, in the fifties and sixties railways were being laid down throughout the country. At the main terminal cities there were large colonies of Anglo-Indians—people of mixed ancestry but mostly of English culture. They spoke English. Taylor felt that they were the natural evangelists of

India and that they constituted on the spot a ready-made source for missionaries. Furthermore, since many members of this community had good jobs in the railways and in telegraphy, they had means to support their own ministry as well as to carry on work among the Indians. Traditionally, these people were related to the Church of England, which did not always meet their emotional needs. Many were soundly converted and joined the Methodists.

During his four years of evangelistic campaigns, Taylor concentrated on these centers, a mark of his strategy. We can follow him from city to city: Bombay, Poona, Calcutta, Hyderabad, Madras, Bangalore, and others. Not only Anglo-Indians but many English were converted and were in these centers organized into English-speaking churches—most of which continue to the present.

Among his converts were some outstanding men, a number of whom became effective preachers. He also brought out missionaries from America as pastors for his congregations—fifty of them over a period of a few years.

In 1872 Taylor petitioned the General Conference to grant a provisional charter for the Bombay Conference. This was not done, it being regarded preposterous that a sufficient foundation could have been laid in so short a time. Nevertheless the next year a Bombay and Bengal Mission was established under Taylor's superintendency, and in 1876 the General Conference did approve the organization of a South India Conference, covering all of India outside the original field selected by Butler. This became the "mother of conferences" for from it were formed in succession over a period of fifty years the Bengal (1888), Bombay (1892), Northwest India (now Delhi, 1893), Central Provinces (now Madhya Pradesh, 1904), Lucknow (1921), Gujarat (1922), Indus River (1926), Hyderabad (1926) Conferences, and a South India Conference itself continues. The original field is now known as the North India Conference.

The tremendous toil involved in this growth can well be imagined. There is romance in it all, regarding which only two incidents will be recounted. In 1885 the Rev. and Mrs. S. P. Jacobs, "Taylor" missionaries from Ohio, first went to Gulbarga in Hyderabad State. Having no residence, they lived in a mausoleum-like building, meant for a Muslim tomb. Even from this place they were later driven by robbers who used it as a hide-out. In any case, the power of the gospel cannot be contained within the walls of a tomb! As from the first Christian tomb new life and salvation broke forth in the person of Jesus, so the gospel broke out of these unpromising surroundings. If one were today to draw a circle perhaps a hundred miles in radius around the tomb, at least a hundred thousand Methodists would be found living inside the circle. The 1952 session of the South India Annual Conference was held in a palace not a mile from that tomb! It is reminiscent of the New Testament, when Paul could write to the Philippians, "All the saints salute you, especially they that are of Caesar's household." Thirty years from tomb to palace! In South India it took a bit longer.

Of similar interest is the record of the "Twelve Apostles." Around the turn of the century, Bishops Warne, Thoburn, and Parker recruited twelve stalwart single men who were given the above designation. Among them were Karl E. Anderson, Robert I. Fawcett, Mott Keislar, and Brenton T. Badley, afterwards bishop. Bishop Badley once told the writer that eleven of these twelve completed full terms of missionary service, totalling in all some three hundred and ninety years!

A few words must be given here about the work of the Methodist Protestant Church in India. Its activity was centered in only one district in and about Dhulia, approximately two hundred miles northeast of Bombay. Just before 1900 a Methodist Protestant layman encouraged attendants at a camp meeting in Louisiana to support two missionaries in India. They were Miss Mattie Long who was in charge of a girls' school and Miss Florence Williams, an evangelistic worker. In

1916 the Board of Foreign Missions of the Methodist Protestant Church officially undertook responsibility for the station. Later an orphanage, a hospital, and a farm settlement were started. In 1939 the work of the Bombay Conference was related to this work.

The former Methodist Episcopal Church, South, did not work in the India field. A number of notable missionaries from that branch of the church did, however, serve in Southern Asia even before unification.

Mass Movements

It has been indicated that at least 80 per cent of the Protestants of India are estimated to be of depressed class origin. The means by which they came into the church was by mass movements. This term is inadequate; perhaps group or peoples' movement would be better. From early days whole caste groups in certain areas responded to the preaching of the first Catholic missionaries. Beginning in the early 1800's a similar development took place in several Protestant fields in South India. The story of this whole development is simply told by Bishop J. Waskom Pickett, who has studied the process thoroughly, in his splendid book, *Christ's Way to India's Heart*.

Undoubtedly the missionaries would have been gratified by a larger response from the higher caste groups and the more educated. The securing of these folk would naturally suggest that from them the blessings of the gospel would have spread throughout society. In general, however, such groups were precisely the ones who did *not* respond, for lack of a deep sense of need. As Jesus said, "They that are whole have no need for a physician, but they that are sick." (Mark 2:17).

In actual fact the missionary did not find the front door open, but rather the back door, as it were. In North India by 1861 there was a response among the Mazabhi Sikhs. These were folk of outcaste origin who had previously accepted the religion of the Sikhs but were not admitted into the social structure of that religion. Most of them subsequently became Christians. By 1868 there was great interest on the part of the Sweepers, to be followed, beginning about 1881, by the Chamars, traditional leather-workers. Much later similar developments took place in other parts of the Methodist field.

The mass movements followed the natural social organization of the people—along caste lines. Often all the people of a particular depressed class group living in one village would enter the church. Their baptism was preceded usually by a longer or shorter period of instruction in basic Christian beliefs and practices. The movement would spread from village to village as the word would be shared with relatives or fellows of his caste near by. Something fairly close to it is found in recent efforts in the West at present in "guild evangelism"—doctors among doctors, lawyers among lawyers.

Mass movements are often regarded with doubt by Westerners. Here we have a long tradition of individualism, especially in religion. We are forgetful that in Northern Europe Christianity spread in exactly the same way, with the conversion of whole tribes. From a fairly elementary or primitive background the conversion process seems to be as Paul described it, ". . . ye turned unto God from idols, to serve a living and true God" (I Thess. 1:9). The original turning from non-Christian beliefs must, of course, be followed by continued teaching and pastoral care. Often this follow-up has been inadequate.

In contrast to our individual approach, the sense of the group, whether family or caste, has traditionally been very strong in India. Once the writer spoke to an educated Hindu during the course of a train journey, asking if he were a member of the Congress Party. His surprising answer was: "No, my brother is, however. He has the politics of the family. We vote as he says." He was a member of a "joint family," several related families, as we think of them, living under one roof under the direction of the father or eldest brother. A villager often uses the plural pronoun because of this group sense.

Hence, a group decision is often reached in a perfectly natural way.

Dr. Latourette says that the group approach "was at once the opportunity, the glory, and the acute problem of the Church in India." [4] The problem of motive arises and it was often a mixture between the spiritual, the economic, the social. There is also the problem of adequate pastoral care. Writing of this problem a pioneer missionary, the Rev. P. M. Buck, said:

"Perhaps the chief peril that faces us is an unchristianized Christianity. Multitudes await the nominal acceptance of the gospel; but to win them to the real life that is in Christ and to nourish them up into the full stature of manhood is a very different matter. The number reaching the new life that the Spirit imparts must determine all worthy success." [5]

Tremendous efforts were expended to give pastoral care and to train workers adequate to such a task.

With all of its faults, there can be no doubt that there was often a tremendous transformation in the lives of many of these people. This was at times so striking as to awaken the interest of caste Hindus in the gospel. Furthermore, from these villages has come a steady stream of young people to Christian schools in urban centers where they have formed the substantial Christian congregations to be found there. One classic story of an aspect of this transformation is cited of the Brahmin who asked a Christian of outcaste origin: "What has Christianity done for you?" The reply was: "Well, for one thing, I am no longer afraid of you." Another testimony is from a prominent Hindu leader who is openly unsympathetic with Christian evangelism: "One thing I will say: if these missionaries get hold of one from the low-castes, they make a man of him!"

Many, many examples of striking Christian characters from

---

[4] *A History of the Expansion of Christianity,* Vol. VI, K. S. Latourette, New York: Harper and Bros., 1939, p. 207.

[5] From a diary of P. M. Buck, quoted by his daughter, Mrs. J. H. Wilkie, in a manuscript and used with her permission.

this background might be given. None is more impressive than Narsamma. For years she was a priestess of a shrine to the smallpox goddess in the village of Kohir in Hyderabad State. Many of the outcaste folk were her followers. Gradually they began to respond to the Christian message which was being preached there. Seeing this as a loss to her economically and in prestige, she opposed the movement vehemently. Finally she listened to the preaching and upon hearing of the change in the lives of her relatives, she too became a seeker. In 1909 she was converted, and for her it was a marvelous change. She became a radiant person, the most outstanding Christian of the district, for years a powerful evangelist who persuaded many to dedicate themselves to Jesus Christ. A stone of her former shrine to the smallpox goddess is now part of the altar of the church in Kohir.

Mass movements do not constitute merely a success story. There have been numerous failures too. In 1935 Dr. B. R. Ambedkar, a principal leader of untouchables, in a speech renounced Hinduism, the religion of his birth, and invited his followers to do likewise. There was much speculation at the time as to whether or not there might be an even greater influx into the church of this group, a development for which the church was ill prepared. About that time the great Bishop of Dornakal, Azariah, conferred with Ambedkar. The latter said in substance, "If you are suggesting that my people should unite with the church, with *which* church shall they unite?" Thus he pointed to the scandal of our divisions. Thereafter Bishop Azariah was more than ever convinced that Christian unity was not an elective but a necessity for the church in India.

In 1946 in Delhi a visitor called on Dr. Ambedkar, with whom he had been acquainted for a number of years. At that time Dr. Ambedkar was Minister of Labor in the Indian Cabinet. While waiting for him at his residence his secretary showed the visitor about the house. There were two large living rooms with an office in between. Above the mantlepiece in one room was a picture of Buddha, an Indian. Above the mantle-piece in the other was a picture of Christ. Above the desk in the study was a picture of "Christ before Pilate," one of the original prints. When Dr. Ambedkar came out, the visitor took him on a tour of his own house to view in turn these three pictures. As they stood finally before the latter picture, the trial scene, the acquaintance asked: "Dr. Ambedkar, isn't that about where you stand, thinking what you will do with Jesus?" He replied: "Yes, I guess you're about right."

Four years later the visitor called at his office again. Dr. Ambedkar was then Law Minister of the Cabinet, equivalent to our Attorney General. The visitor recalled the earlier scene. Dr. Ambedkar remembered the occasion. Then he said, "You may be interested to know that last week I became a Buddhist!"

A Hundred Years Old

Soon Methodism in India will have completed a hundred years. There are shadows, but on the whole it has been a glorious period. A committee in India is working hard to plan an adequate celebration; and, more important, the church is aiming at reaching certain goals by that time. It desires especially to increase support locally for its work and is planning other creative undertakings.

Methodism in Southern Asia has always been creative. New departures were undertaken in response to needs which arose. For example, the District Conference was originated in North India. Since some districts were fairly widely separated from others and had peculiar problems and since district workers required periods of careful instruction, the District Conference was devised first of all in 1862 to meet the need. It has spread throughout Methodism.

Likewise the Central Conference originated in India. With the spread of Methodism throughout much of the country under Taylor, some device of co-ordination and mutual counsel was necessary. Such a joint conference was first held in Allahabad in 1881. It was approved by the General Conference of the Methodist Episcopal Church in 1884 and was soon afterwards instituted in other parts of the world. It afforded a pattern for the Jurisdictional Conference in the reunion of Methodism in 1939.

It was a memorial from the Bengal Conference to the General Conference of 1888 that resulted in the founding of a deaconess movement in Methodism. Thus Southern Asia has in a number of ways exerted influence throughout the denomination.

From the very beginning leadership by Indians was promoted. At an early date Indians were made annual conference members. Soon Indian district superintendents appeared. Today in every realm Indian leadership is the rule, with missionaries in most cases working under the direction of their Indian colleagues. Both Bishop Shot K. Mondol, elected by the Central Conference of 1940-41, and Bishop John A. Subhan, elected four years later, are giving outstanding episcopal leadership. The latter is probably the only one in Christian history, born a Muslim, to become a bishop. Constant attention needs to be given to housing and other working conditions if talented Indians are to continue to be attracted to church-related vocations.

Mention must be made of the more than one hundred Crusade Scholars who have come to the United States from India and Pakistan. They have studied from Boston University to the University of Southern California; from Scarritt to Garrett; from Iliff to Illinois Wesleyan. Their fields of study, aside from theology and religious education, have ranged from business administration to surgery, from home economics to nuclear physics. To them countless churches and members in America have opened their hearts and their homes. They, with the other Crusade Scholars from two score lands, have in turn lifted our spirits and have aided us in seeing Jesus Christ through other eyes. Moreover, the great majority have served the church in some capacity upon their return.

The international character of the development of the Methodist Church in Southern Asia must be stressed. Aside from Indians and Anglo-Indians, workers of the following nationalities have served in the church in India: Americans, Scots, English, Irish, Canadians, Germans, Swiss, Swedish, Danish, Norwegians, Finnish, Peruvian. During World War II temporary helpers, either missionaries or nationals, came from Burma, Malaya, Sumatra, Japan, China, the Philippines, Korea, North Africa. Moreover from the United States have come missionaries of a variety of backgrounds: Negroes, Niseis, Italian- and Greek-Americans. All these have contributed toward the dream of William Butler, still unrealized, that "India shall yet be one of the brightest gems in the diadem of Christ."

CHAPTER V

THE FACE OF METHODISM IN INDIA

THE FACE of Indian Methodism is a composite face. It is made up of the hosts of men and women who have labored to establish a church. For building a church consists not merely of programs, nor of institutions nor of plans, but largely of people—people with a passion to share a common love for Jesus Christ. Who were some of those who helped to build Indian Methodism?

JAMES MILLS THOBURN (*1836-1922*)

If a movement is the "lengthened shadow of a man," then more than to any other individual is Methodism in Southern Asia indebted to Bishop James M. Thoburn. For over half a century he was intimately associated with every aspect of the work there. He was of the same small stature as Wesley and Asbury, and his gifted personality combined abilities as evangelist, writer, Christian statesman, and practical mystic.

Born of Irish-American parents in St. Clairsville, Ohio, he received his training at Allegheny College. While there he was converted and called to the ministry. His first charge yielded an annual salary of $100 a year. As a young man he was strongly impressed that he should some day become a missionary. Later he became so clear about this that he went to ask the advice of his presiding elder. Meanwhile the presiding elder was making his way to Thoburn with the proposal that he become a recruit for India. Thus confirmed, he joined a party of five other new missionaries who in the fall of 1859 arrived in Calcutta to reinforce William Butler.

When Thoburn arrived on the field, there were thirteen enrolled Methodists in India. When he retired in 1908, there were over 200,000. Toward that growth he was a very active agent.

For one thing, he advocated a policy of expansion. In this he was stimulated by William Taylor. Butler, for his part, believed in a policy of concentration—to that part of North India now known as Uttar Pradesh. Thoburn accepted preaching engagements at Kanpur on the further shore of the Ganges. When he secured approval for this move, he called it "crossing the Indian Rubicon." Soon, in 1874, he became one of Taylor's self-supporting missionaries, serving with great effectiveness in Calcutta for fourteen years. An English-speaking church there today bears his name.

Thoburn's vision led him to Burma, where he launched Methodism in 1879. He began by evangelistic services, followed by organizing a small congregation which became the center of further activity. He shared with Taylor and Wesley the ability to organize those who were converted so that effort might not be lost. Leaving the Rev. John E. Robinson in charge, he returned to Calcutta. Robinson later became a bishop.

When Bishop John F. Hurst visited India in 1883 he suggested to Thoburn the strategic importance of Singapore through which he had just passed. The latter had himself long thought that Methodism should extend to Malaya. In February, 1885, Dr. and Mrs. Thoburn, together with the Rev. W. F. Oldham, sailed from Calcutta. Having insufficient funds, they stopped at Rangoon to raise the rest of their passage money among Methodist friends. At Singapore, Methodism was launched on the same pattern used in Burma six years earlier. Singapore became a part of the Rangoon District of the South India Conference! Oldham, of Anglo-Indian origin, remained as an effective self-supporting pastor, later to become a missionary bishop, a mission board secretary, a General Superintendent.

Thoburn was elected in 1888 as the first missionary bishop for Southern Asia. In March, 1899, he proceeded to Manila. He pioneered in establishing Methodism there, within a few

months of the defeat of the Spanish by Admiral Dewey. This
development had also been in his mind for years. He placed
the Rev. Homer C. Stuntz in charge there. He, too, was to
become a bishop.

By this time far-flung Southern Asia Methodism was using
thirty-seven languages!

Furthermore, Bishop Thoburn was the first leader who saw
clearly the strategic importance of mass movements in North
India. While others were skeptical, he said: "So far as the possibility of elevating these Indian people of low caste is concerned,
I venture to affirm that the problem has already been solved." [1]

Thoburn was largely responsible for the development of
Special Gifts for Methodist mission projects. He stimulated
this program while speaking at Northfield in 1890 at the invitation of Dwight L. Moody. After he had described the great
opportunities in the mass movement areas, he was asked how
much the annual support of a single pastor-teacher among
these people would be. He estimated $30 a year. Support for
a thousand of these workers was subscribed on the spot, Moody
and Sankey each sponsoring one. A young student, Sherwood
Eddy, was present and assumed the support of one preacher
then and two others later on. Thereafter such "specials" often
amounted to $50,000 a year for Thoburn's work.

Dr. John R. Mott regarded Thoburn as one of the ablest
Christian statesmen in history. He was always "devising a plan."
He was an able interpreter of India and gifted spokesman for
India. He wrote ten books concerning his work, some of them of
great value even today.

Something of Bishop Thoburn's prophetic vision and spirit
can be seen in this statement during the golden jubilee of Indian
Methodism in 1906:

---

[1] *India and Malaysia,* James M. Thoburn, New York: Hunt and Eaton,
1892, p. 405.

"The time is auspicious, and the missionaries of India should not lose a day, or an hour, in sounding the trumpet for a great forward movement. India is to be won for Christ, and the greatest movement ever attempted in the history of Christianity is now at hand. *Nothing since the day of Pentecost* has equaled the present opportunity. The old may rejoice that they have lived to see this day; but the young may rejoice still more in the hope of seeing a day when a million souls will be found in North India, a million in West India, a million in Burma, and still a million more in South India. A million? Why not ten millions? Why not the Christian conquest of India?" [2]

His vision was greater than accomplishment to the present. Was his vision too large or is our effort too small?

ISABELLA THOBURN (*1840-1901*) [3]

A recent visitor from America said: "All the proof I'd ever need that missions are worth while is to walk one day through an Indian village and the next through Isabella Thoburn College. Not a word need be said. It's all right there."

That statement is the latest tribute to Isabella Thoburn, a missionary of ceaseless labor and unwavering purpose. A forerunner of the thousands of single women missionaries of The Methodist Church, she has not been surpassed by any of them.

She shared the same family heritage as Bishop Thoburn. In her youth Isabella Thoburn was not of unusual religious bent. She became deeply religious but was never strongly vocal about it. Though she never doubted the *fact* of her conversion, she did not know the *date* of it.

Trained as an educator, she came to India partly at the invitation of her brother who had written to her using, of all things, a quill pen made from a vulture's feather. She and Dr.

---

[2] *Indian Mission Jubilee,* ed. Frederick B. Price, Methodist Publishing House, Calcutta, 1907, p. 252.

[3] For much of this sketch the writer is indebted to Bishop Thoburn's biography of his sister, *Life of Isabella Thoburn,* New York: Eaton and Mains, 1903.

Clara A. Swain were appointed the first missionaries of the newly organized Woman's Foreign Missionary Society. Together they sailed for India and on January 7, 1870, were met in Bombay by George Bowen.

Isabella Thoburn was at home in India from the first. "I have never felt homesick since I knew God to be my Father," she said. She always saw the good in India: the friendliness, the natural beauty, the tender affection of parent toward child, the smiling hill women.

It was characteristic of her to lose no time, so three months after arriving in India she launched a girls' school in Lucknow where her brother was then presiding elder. Only six girls were there at the start. They were of mixed background—another principle of hers. She wrote some years later: "To work for and with all classes of people, we must be one with all, and belong to no class ourselves, which will sometimes mean that we must become low-caste." Her enthusiasm for educating girls was not without opposition. She frequently had to remind Indian preachers: "No people ever rise higher . . . than the point to which they elevate their women."

A year later, in 1871, she purchased the splendid site of Lal Bagh or "Ruby Garden" in the heart of Lucknow. The transaction was completed by the transfer of fourteen bags, each containing one thousand silver rupees brought in a tonga to the former owner. This was the first location of the college which now bears Miss Thoburn's name, founded in 1886, the first college for women in all Asia. It was her greatest single contribution. She was clear that the establishment of this institution was the will of God. Visitors at Lal Bagh today are invited to sit in Miss Thoburn's chair.

Yet Isabella Thoburn found time for other activities than her school. She pioneered in Sunday schools for hundreds of non-Christian girls in Lucknow. She was always caring for the sick. She found time to teach Hindustani to the wife of a viceroy,

Lady Dufferin. She helped to found the deaconess movement in the Methodist Church and was herself one of the first deaconesses. She wrote one book, many articles and speeches and was editor of a Hindustani magazine for Christian women. She was in demand as a speaker both in India and at home. Though she did not like to appear in public, she made important addresses at the three largest missionary conferences of her day.

Her whole life was a testimony to the fact that she was eminently practical. She had confidence in the ability of Indian women, so spent herself for their development.

Isabella Thoburn had a philosophy of humble Christian service, of which her life was a demonstration. She expressed it in many ways: "When we only seek eminence and position, how few avenues are open! When we seek service, how many—all with wide gates, and loud calls, and pleading invitations, to come where work, and room, and reward await all!" To a missionary candidate: "You say you are not sure of the call because you are conscious of being so unworthy. If you felt yourself worthy, I should doubt you. . . . Every missionary candidate should learn by heart, in the deepest sense, that golden thirteenth chapter of First Corinthians." When her friend Lilavati Singh was pondering Christian work, Isabella told her: "If you once get the taste for this service, nothing else will satisfy you."

Lilavati Singh accompanied Miss Thoburn to America in 1900. It was while there that former President Benjamin Harrison remarked of her: "If I had given a million dollars to foreign missions, and was assured that no result had come from it all except the evolution of one such woman as that, I should feel amply repaid for my expenditure."

After Isabella Thoburn died of cholera in Lucknow in 1901, Lilavati said of her: ". . . just as Jesus came to show us the Father, she had come to show us Jesus." No missionary could do more, nor is called to do anything less.

GEORGE BOWEN *(1816-1888)* [4]

Though not nearly so well known as he deserves, George Bowen was one of the most remarkable men of the 19th century. In his character he combined something of the spiritual qualities of St. Paul, St. Augustine, and St. Francis. William Taylor said of him, "If the Roman Catholics had him, they would canonize him as a saint." [5]

George Bowen was born in New England in 1816 into a privileged family, but one singularly lacking in qualities which might foster sainthood. He was brilliant to the point of genius but, after his twelfth year, largely self-educated. He was familiar with a number of languages; was widely read; was a talented pianist. By the time he was twenty he had written several tragedies in blank verse, one of which was published.

As a young man Bowen was a skeptic and lived a reckless life. His extensive travel on the Continent was sprinkled with love affairs and gay night life. He was possessed at that period of a violent temper. For a period he carried a pistol, intending to rid society of a man who had offended him. He admits having once written an anonymous letter to President Andrew Jackson threatening to shoot him if he did not change a policy. He was alarmed when the letter was published. Such was the unlikely background for a saint.

In 1844 after the tragic death of the girl he loved he was converted. Partly this developed from reading her Bible. One night he wrote, almost unwillingly:

"If there is One above all who notices the desires of men, I wish that He would take note of this fact, that if it please Him to make known His will concerning me, I shall think it my highest privilege to do that will, whatever it may be and whatever it may involve." [6]

---

[4] The principal source book on Bowen is Robert E. Speer's *George Bowen of Bombay*, printed privately 1938.

[5] *Four Years' Campaign in India,* William Taylor, New York: Phillips and Hunt, 1875, p. 12.

[6] Robert E. Speer, *op. cit.,* p. 72.

Soon afterward he had been transformed into a convinced and Biblical Christian. His conversion was as radical as Saul's at Damascus, but was spread over a longer period. The self-centered egotist became a Christ-centered person.

Following three years at Union Theological Seminary in New York, he was accepted as a missionary by the American Board (Congregational) and in 1847 sailed for India. He never again returned to his homeland. The trip out required six months, during which time he worked with the sailors and began to learn Marathi.

In Bombay he committed himself without restraint to missionary effort. He wrote: "I want to have Christ walking about the streets of Bombay as He did about those of Jerusalem, and living among this people as He did among the Jews." [7] This desire he fulfilled to a large extent in his own life.

Bowen's procedure in those days was preaching on the streets. He also sold and distributed tracts and Gospel portions. At times he was assaulted by mobs. They would bowl him over, destroy the literature, throw mud or stones at him, and generally abuse him. All this he took in good spirit. He deeply felt, however, what seemed to be a general rejection of the gospel.

Such circumstances convinced him that people must be shocked into acceptance. This would best be done by a miracle. He recalled the miracle-working power of apostolic days. On this subject he studied, meditated, and prayed for a long time. Finally on the streets of Bombay he attempted a miracle. It was the opening of the eyes of a blind man. The attempt was a miserable failure and crushed Bowen inwardly. From this he recovered and it is to the credit of his friends as well as the Indian crowds that they never mentioned his failure. But although Bowen had failed in this proposed miracle, he launched forth on a far more convincing one—the miracle of a saintly life.

---

[7] *Ibid.,* p. 140.

He then cultivated a life of extreme poverty. This he did not advocate for others. He felt that it was Scriptural and therefore renounced his missionary salary, supporting himself by tutoring for an hour a day. He lived on the equivalent of about five dollars a month. Although he was poor, he was rich. People always wanted to do things for him but he refused. Clothes and furniture given to him he usually gave away. Having nothing, all things were his, for he could immediately secure any amount of money he desired for any cause.

He writes: "Probably the holiest man in the world is he who retains most keenly and unceasingly the sense of his liability to sin. I desire to be that man."

Meanwhile he continued his missionary efforts. He was a founder in 1850 of the *Guardian* of Bombay and its distinguished editor until his death. By many it was regarded as the most remarkable religious paper in the world at that time. He was secretary of the Bombay Tract and Book Society and for a time principal of a school. Daily he continued street preaching and pastoral work. He found time to write several books; three of them are devotional classics. In 1872 he joined the Methodists as one of William Taylor's preachers.

As the years went by he was increasingly known and loved by everyone in the city. His striking appearance was one of the sights in the streets. People of all stations of life respected him and came to him. The low-caste Hindu, the Brahmin, the Muslim, the Parsee, the other missionaries, the poor Anglo-Indian, Government officials, the Governor—all were his friends. When the Prince of Wales came to India, he paid a call on Bowen and brought to him the special regards of his mother, Queen Victoria. By many Indians it was said of him, "There is a man that is like Jesus Christ."

He was known as the "White Yogi" or saint. One friend writes of him:

"The White Yogi differed from other saints of church and heathen history in many respects. He was not sour or sanctimonious. He was not austere or critical. He never complained of other people's style of living. He went, like Jesus, gladly to the feasts and festivals of rich and poor alike. In palace and hut George Bowen was always a welcome guest, ready by any means in his power to contribute to the joys of young and old."

It is hardly safe to judge a man's work by results, for they are always both tangible and intangible. If George Bowen were to be judged by the number of converts, he was a failure. He himself felt this keenly. There were those who professed to have been converted under his ministry. Other Christians were deepened by contact with his spiritual radiance. One of his colleagues stated that he was very unskillful at "drawing in the net."

When Bowen died, all Bombay mourned. Until recent years on the anniversary of his death, a Hindu was seen to bring fresh flowers to George Bowen's grave. A Methodist church in Bombay is named as a memorial to him.

PHOEBE ROWE (1856-1898)

As one reads records and diaries of early Indian Methodism in North India, he is constantly meeting with the name of Phoebe Rowe. Almost always is she referred to as "saintly." In a simple and humble way she was a counterpart of George Bowen. A healthy church gives rise constantly to characters of outstanding Christlikeness, who in turn contribute to the further health of the church.

Phoebe Rowe was born at Allahabad. As an Anglo-Indian she is representative of many others of her people who have made outstanding contributions to the church, such as William F. Oldham, Grace Stephens, Ruth Partridge, Dennis Osborne and others. She combined the gentleness and devotion of her Indian mother and the integrity of her Scots father, under whose personal direction she was educated.

She was a girl in her teens when she came to the Lal Bagh School in Lucknow which Isabella Thoburn had opened in

1870. For ten years that was her home and there she taught.
Her stamp on the institution was evident for years. Miss Thoburn could say of her: "Miss Rowe did not mold from without,
but implanted character in her pupils. She had the rare power
of seeing the best possibilities of each nature, and so developed
them that the evil had not room to grow, but gave place to the
good." [8] Her own character was such that she called forth a
nobleness in others.

Phoebe had an unforgettably attractive singing voice in both
Hindustani and English. This gift she employed effectively, and
it was the gateway to evangelistic work in which she soon was
engaged constantly. In her Bible she wrote: "The Lord being
my helper, I will comfort the feeble-minded, support the weak,
be patient toward all." [9] These words became the key of her
life and work.

She possessed in marked degree a simplicity of faith. Once
seeking deliverance from pride and selfishness, more evident
to her than to others, she says: "I prepared to struggle; but when
I knelt beside my bed and looked up, I saw the face of my
Heavenly Father, and the work was done." [10]

Again she writes: "Jesus has come to my heart in a new way
through his Word. I have spent more time with my Bible, and
it has been a blessing to me, as well as to those to whom I
talk." [11]

Though she was of mystical bent, the note of simplicity was
always there. Of guidance she said: "The opinion of good
people about my duty is the only guidance I ever receive." Again
she remarked: "How many friends I found in finding the
Lord."

As is common with folk of her type, she had a deep esthetic

[8] *Phoebe Rowe*, Isabella Thoburn, New York: Eaton and Mains, 1899, p. 18.
[9] *Ibid.*, p. 33.
[10] *Ibid.*, p. 21.
[11] *Ibid.*, p. 129.

sense. Her letters and diary are full of such entries as: "What a beautiful world this is, and how full of kind hearts! Why do I get more than my share of it all." "I have been to Delhi, and lost my heart to it. No place I ever saw affected me like this Moti Masjid (the Pearl Mosque) . . . I wanted to get down on my face and pray." In camp: "The light and shade through the mango trees make a pretty carpet for the place chosen for our service, while the boughs overhead form a bower, and the birds will join in the singing." "I can see the roses and heliotrope at Lal Bagh, and all the green vines that decorate the room, and I can smell the coffee that was passed around . . ."

In view of her effectiveness as an evangelist she was appointed in 1882 to missionary status—the first Indian woman to be so recognized. Bishop Thoburn also recognized her as the first Indian deaconess. She was tireless as an itinerant village evangelist, being appointed at one time or another in most of the principal stations in the North India Conference. Often she recorded incidents of great interest. Once an old Muslim threatened to accuse her on judgment day if she did not send a teacher to his village. A heartbreaking experience was the witnessing a zealous village preacher breaking a Hindu idol to show it was powerless. Unfortunately that night he died of a stroke, which seemed to the onlookers the vengeance of the goddess.

Finally she strained her weak body more than it could bear. She died in Naini Tal of diphtheria.

In true humility she always discounted her effect on others. Her friends could say of her, however: "She was the loveliest, purest spirit I ever knew." "Her character was a masterpiece in the studies of grace." "She was like Him and lived like Him here." "Phoebe was a saint; we all knew it." Bishop Thoburn wrote: "The possibility of holy living, the nature of entire consecration, the value of a blameless life, the nature of unquestioning faith: all these things will remain as a rich possession to our mission for many years in connection with the memory of her sainted life." [12]

JASHWANT RAO CHITAMBAR *(1879-1940)*

Bishop J. R. Chitambar became a familiar personality in the United States during his many visits here. His tall, erect figure was made even more striking by the Pathan headdress he wore, marking him as an Indian. He was outstanding in his generation.

Few who met him ever forgot him. Yet it was not just Bishop Chitambar one remembered, but the Master whom he served. His motto was Scriptural: "That in all things He might have the pre-eminence." Those words continued as the theme of his widow, Satyavati Singh Chitambar, to this day. He translated into happy Urdu the chorus, "Let the Beauty of Jesus Be Seen in Me." Everywhere he went he sang it. It was his marching song. The words were fulfilled in him.

As is the case with all able men, he had many facets to his character. He was an effective writer. Among other things he wrote a biography of Mahatma Gandhi. He revised and improved an Urdu dictionary. For years he was editor of the Hindustani Methodist periodical. To his credit is the translation of a number of hymns. Frequently he was called upon to translate from English the addresses of visiting dignitaries. It had to be poor speech indeed if it were not rendered by him effectively into Hindustani. He could listen to a whole address; then translate it without missing a thing. His administrative ability was outstanding. He was a good teacher. Above all he was a powerful evangelistic preacher.

J. R. Chitambar was the son of a Methodist preacher. His father had been in his youth a Brahmin from the proud Mahratta country of Western India. When the father became a Christian, he lost his inheritance and moved to the north.

---

[12] *Ibid.*, p. 171.

The son went in his youth to the Centennial Methodist High School in Lucknow, where he was converted and challenged later to Christian life service by John R. Mott. Then he studied at Lucknow Christian College. He was the first degree student to attend Bareilly Seminary, from which he was graduated in 1903.

Then followed a succession of appointments of increasing responsibility: teacher at Bareilly, headmaster of the Centennial High School. While there he had a tremendous influence on the boys, with thirty-four of them at one time headed for the ministry. Along the way, he was a delegate to a World Student Conference in Tokyo; another in Washington, D. C.; a delegate to the famous Missionary Conference in Edinburgh in 1910. Then came service as a district superintendent, as general secretary of the Epworth League throughout India, as executive secretary of the Board of Home and Foreign Missions organized in India, as principal of Lucknow Christian College. Finally, in 1930 he was elected bishop, the first Indian to fill that office in our church. This he did with distinction and credit to his fellow countrymen.

The Chitambars' home was always a Christian home at its best. Prayer was at the heart of it. Mrs. Chitambar, an outstanding person in her own right, always worked in closest support of her husband's efforts. Their family is a tribute to them both. The eldest daughter teaches music at Isabella Thoburn College. A second daughter, long a teacher, is now the wife of a doctor. The eldest son is active in social welfare work in industry. The second is a leader and pioneer in civil aviation in India. Another son is surgeon at the Methodist hospital at Nadiad in Gujarat, developing an enviable reputation throughout the country in his profession. The youngest son is in charge of the Research and Extension Department of Allahabad Agricultural Institute.

Bishop Chitambar was a "happy warrior," renowned for his good humor. He liked nothing better than to tell a story on himself. For example, "During a visit to the United States, I was waiting," he said, "for a train and noted a lady who apparently was waiting for the same train. She walked past me several times, evidently interested by my Indian costume and head-dress. Just as the train was coming in she mustered up courage to speak to me and asked, 'And where do you come from?' I replied, 'I am from India.' 'There!' she exclaimed 'I just knew you were from somewhere!' "

The warrior's earthly path came to an end in September, 1940. He had just returned to India exhausted from America, following General Conference of that year. To describe him those who paid tribute used the terms "generous," "fruitful," "honest," "full of love for people," "unsparing in work." One of his episcopal colleagues wrote:

"Bishop Chitambar was notable as an educator and an administrator but in the judgment of many of his brethren his noblest service was rendered in preaching. He was at his best in the pulpit and his best was exceedingly good. Whether speaking in Urdu, Hindi or English he was fluent and forceful, preaching always with passion and power. His expositions of the Scripture were clear, his illustrations apt and illuminating and his applications to the life-situations of his hearers were arresting and persuasive. His appeals, whether to the mind, the conscience or the emotions, were effective to a degree unfortunately attained by relatively few ministers." [13]

Bishop Chitambar brought self-respect in eminent degree to Indian Methodists. He demonstrated clearly the capacity of Indians within the church to give effective leadership, too little recognized before his time. Many are following in his train.

SARAH CHAKKO *(1905-1954)* [14]

Sarah Chakko was beautiful. She did not know it; that added to her charm. She had that grace of manner and carriage charac-

---

[13] Bishop J. Waskom Pickett, quoted in *The Making of a Bishop*, B. T. Badley, Lucknow: Lucknow Publishing House, 1942, pp. 58-9.

[14] Aside from personal reminiscences, the author is indebted in this sketch to the memorial number of the Chand Bagh *Chronicle*, published by Isabella Thoburn College, April, 1954, edited by Marjorie Dimmitt.

teristic of so many Indian women. But hers was an inner grace and beauty of spirit with which few anywhere are endowed. All that this means was a part of her contribution to Methodism in Southern Asia—and, indeed, to the whole church.

What was the secret of this inner beauty with its outward reflection? For one thing it was her splendid family heritage. She had the good fortune to be a part of a large family with five sisters and four brothers. In her beloved land of Travancore she ·was born in a little village on February 13, 1905. The Christians of Travancore are mature people, so that poise was a part of her natural endowment. Her father was a Commissioner of Police in Cochin State. Reading of her mother, one is reminded of Susanna Wesley. Even in India where family ties can be close and relationships beautiful, here was an outstanding family.

Then there was her Christian training, first in the home; then in Christian schools; then in her church. Sarah was not a Methodist. She always remained a member of the ancient Orthodox Syrian Church of her childhood, though in Lucknow she regularly attended a Methodist service. She was deeply stamped as a child of the church.

She demonstrated an unswerving purpose in life. Soon after college graduation it became her clear interest to be an educator. Marriage and a possible career in medicine were set aside. Her great skills in education helped to guide Isabella Thoburn College through the post-war days and the early years of independence. Her counsel was widely sought by other educators.

Sarah Chakko had consummate skill in human relations. Because she knew how to approach others, whether government officials or servants, colleagues or students, her fellow countrymen or foreigners, she was in return admired and respected of all. She could handle tense moments with student strikers from a near-by institution or be a fearless witness when some essential Christian point was at stake. She found time to mingle, if necessity demanded, with the great and near great. She had time also to advise a student: "Don't take your work so seriously that criticism breaks you. I was criticized when I was younger, and I felt the way you do—I, too, would have liked to give up, but something inside pushed me on, and I learned a lesson I'll pass on to you. Don't ever expect the reward for service to be expressed in gratitude or appreciation by those among whom you work. The reward lies in what service does to you yourself—the richness, the sympathy, the humaneness it brings you. If you remember this you will get joy out of what you are doing."

She was a hard worker, setting an example for all her fellow workers. She not only administered an important institution but entered actively into its teaching program. During her last year, for example, she taught religion classes and filled a faculty vacancy in physical education. Though she demanded much of others, she spent herself more fully than the rest.

She knew also how to play. The first time the writer ever saw her, she was playing. She entered into sport with the same joyful enthusiasm she showed in everything else. It seemed peculiarly fitting that she should die on the sports field. It was the way she would have had it.

Inspiring confidence as she did, she was called to ever more important service: student Christian leader, college teacher, vice-principal, principal, member of the National Christian Council of India, president of her provincial Christian Council, vice-president of the World YWCA, chairman of the World Council Commission on the Life and Work of Women in the Church, one of six presidents of the World Council of Churches. In an unusual way she stood as a symbol for women and for Asians in ecumenical circles. She always saw herself in such light, discounting the superb personal qualities she possessed for great responsibility.

Upon being designated a World Council of Churches president she said: "It establishes the principle that a woman *can* work in an official capacity in the Orthodox Syrian Church.

There has never been a rule against it, but it never has been done." When a Methodist bishop approached the India secretaries of the Board of Missions inquiring about the appointment of Miss Chakko as a representative of the World Council of Churches, they replied that it was a wonderful idea, but asked if he knew that she was not a Methodist. He didn't care; they wanted Sarah Chakko. That was a tribute to her and to Methodism too!

Suddenly her work was done. Everything she was doing seemed in readiness. Her final chapel talk seemed prophetic; her last class was on the theme of immortality. At a hymn sing two days before her death she selected appropriately, "There is a light upon the mountains."

On that very last morning she wrote the last paragraph of her annual report:

"All through the year, through happy times and difficult times, I have felt the touch of God transforming our problems into opportunities and ever beckoning us onward to greater usefulness. I thank God for His gift of work and the fellowship of saints."

One of her fellow workers, Miss Marjorie Dimmitt, tells of how Sarah as a child had written her name on the walls of the church in her village. Her name is now inscribed on the walls of the Church Universal.

Time would fail one to mention others who by courage, sacrifice, unfailing faithfulness, and constant witness are a part of this story. Some were long ago forgotten. Some are unforgettable. Each one of these touched upon here brought a special gift to the church in Southern Asia and throughout the world. Bishop Thoburn brought limitless vision; Isabella Thoburn brought practical wisdom; George Bowen and Phoebe Rowe, capacity for saintliness; Bishop Chitambar and Sarah Chakko brought both their versatile talents and their Indian heritage. Through such gifts Christ builds His Church!

CHAPTER VI

CLOSE-UP OF INDIAN METHODISM

IN LUKE 8:1 we are reminded that Jesus "went about through cities and villages, preaching and bringing the good tidings of the kingdom of God." Christian missions are an extension of the ministry of Jesus. Thus the Gospel is not only preached but *brought*.

Often the rightful place in the missionary undertaking of medicine or teaching has been challenged. Actually they are co-ordinate parts of one essential task. They are like the fingers of a hand. We may be grateful that the gospel is not merely a "declared word" but an "acted word."

A non-Christian leader in India said the country needed four things: (1) universal education; (2) economic reconstruction; (3) harmony among the various religious communities; (4) a character-producing faith. The church is interested in each of these ends and more.

THE MINISTRY OF HEALING

It has been seen that Indian Methodism early showed an interest in the physical welfare of the people. Jesus' command was "to preach and to heal." Missionaries were naturally concerned that modern medical care be available to new converts, who often had access only to the ancient and unscientific local systems of medicine. Moreover, a ministry of healing was seen as an expression of the life of Christ. There is always an incentive to disinterested service in the name of Christ.

Medical work is forever stimulating the question: "Why?" This question gives opportunity for specific Christian testimony to be given. For example, some colored slides of leprosy work were picked up by a missionary leader in Calcutta at a shop where he had left the films. The Brahmin owner of the shop asked if he might not show some of the pictures on a screen. When he came to the picture of a Christian nurse binding up the foot of a man afflicted with leprosy, he inquired: "What I want to know is the secret of that?" Then a direct testimony was given.

Clara Swain Hospital

This pioneer institution has now grown to a 240-bed institution. First a woman's hospital, it is now general. The original property was the gift of a near-by prince. Aside from grants from Christians in America, a number of additions including a splendid outpatient building have been made possible by the gifts of grateful patients. A chest ward is under the direction of a missionary surgeon who at one time was a tuberculosis patient himself. The staff of doctors at present includes besides Christians, a Sikh, a Parsee, a Hindu, and a Muslim.

The Clara Swain Hospital is one of seven in India and Pakistan where the Methodist Church engages in nurses' training. Laboratory technicians are also trained there. Emphasis has also been given to the preparation of hospital chaplains.

Drs. Charles and Wilma Perrill superintend this remarkable work. Dr. Wilma has fostered the development of the excellent maternity work. In 1941 there were only sixty deliveries. Many of these were complicated cases. There was a tendency, common in that part of the world, for people to go to the hospital only in extreme cases. Thus the idea develops that hospitals are places where people die.

Slowly this has changed, for abnormal deliveries were successful. There was another setback when eleven girl babies were delivered in a row. The word passed around that if an expectant mother went to the hospital, the child would be a girl, not always a welcome sight in these lands. Finally twin boys were delivered by Caesarean section. That seemed to change things. Now there are at least 500 deliveries each year, most of them normal.

Confidence in the hospital has grown in every way since then.

The launching of a dental clinic at Clara Swain Hospital has resulted from the dedication of one missionary couple, Dr. and Mrs. Robert F. Petersen. After receiving his dental degree and serving in the armed forces, he decided to tithe his years of service. Assuming that he would have about thirty years of dental practice he volunteered for three years' service in the mission field; first for Korea, then India.

Not only did the Petersens have the time of their lives, but they shared their lives with India's people. Hardly had he begun practice in Bareilly when a Hindu banker, whose wife had been treated by Dr. Petersen, gave the money for a first-class dental clinic, one of the best in the country. Over two thousand patients were treated the first year. He also began to train dental technicians and hygienists.

Of his service Dr. Petersen writes:

"I wish I could bring to the attention of dentists, dental hygienists, and laboratory technicians the importance of this new field of missionary service, and the countless opportunities available in this service. Some day dentistry will have its Burma Surgeon, its Albert Schweitzer."

Madar Sanatorium

This institution is a union of two earlier tuberculosis institutions, one for men and one for women. It has at present 200 beds. Drs. Sherwood and Marian Hall are in charge. Prior to coming to India in 1941 they had founded a tuberculosis sanatorium in North Korea. Sherwood Hall has the distinction of having introduced tuberculosis Christmas seals into both Korea and India.

No one knows how many active cases of tuberculosis there are in India and Pakistan. It is estimated that a million people die of the disease each year in these lands. The sad lot of refugees from Pakistan together with widespread food shortages increased the incidence of this disease. As one doctor says, "Tuberculosis is not so much a physical disease in India as an economic disease." Madar and similar hospitals under Christian auspices are in response to a deep need.

The latest medical and surgical techniques are available at Madar. A splendid Anglo-Indian surgeon, Dr. J. Thompson Wells, is the principal surgeon, having been trained as a Crusade Scholar in the United States and in India.

Passing through the doors at Madar are patients of all religious communities and many walks of life—a railway official, a Sikh refugee from Pakistan, a preacher, a Hindu classical dancer—only a few from among the many who cannot yet have treatment. The very fact that *some* are receiving care gives hope to the many.

No patient was more attractive than Jacob Masih. Having lost an arm and a leg due to the ravages of this disease, he found a new life at Madar. Seldom did one encounter a more cheerful patient. His room became a chapel; his bed a pulpit; his sermon, a smile and a joyful testimony of his friendship with Christ as healing Saviour. Now recovered, he is a useful Christian.

Raj Kumari Amrit Kaur, the only Christian and the only woman in the Indian Cabinet, regards Madar as one of the finest tubercular hospitals in the country.

All-India Missions Tablet Industry

A unique institution is the All-India Missions Tablet Industry. For more than thirty years it has served mission hospitals throughout the subcontinent. It was founded by the late Dr. H. H. Linn, who was known as the "chief piller" of the church. Tablets are both manufactured and distributed by this industry, together with other types of medicines. It is now being operated under the direction of a son of the founder. In 1920 half a million pills were distributed, whereas in 1953 the number had increased to 35.5 million. Throughout its service it has been self-supporting and moreover has contributed greatly through the active Christian witness which has always been associated with it.

A characteristic of Methodist medical work has been the part played by Indian doctors and nurses. Examples are the work of Drs. Obed and Elizabeth Shantappa, who spent themselves without restraint for years at the hospital in Bidar where the development was literally from a dung heap to an important medical institution. Fortunately their daughter and her husband, both doctors, are today carrying on the tradition. Nearby at Vikarabad, Dr. B. V. Carnaran operates a splendid, though inadequately equipped hospital, giving special emphasis to medical extension work. At Almora, in the Himalayas, Dr. Manohar Masih is in charge of a leprosarium. A government official urged him not to emphasize Christiainity in the treatment of patients. The courageous doctor insisted that emphasis on Christianity must be continued for leprosy was not merely a physical but a spiritual disease.

WITNESSING THROUGH EDUCATION

Christian schools have made a tremendous contribution to Indian life. For years the many Methodist schools have played their part. They are in fact "parochial" schools. They range from nursery schools to the collegiate level.

Under British rule education was largely Western in tone and, at higher levels, instruction was through the medium of English. In 1854 there was established a grant-in-aid system to schools under private auspices. These grants were available on a fixed scale, subject to certain standards of equipment, curriculum, and staff. Though this is contrary to American tradition, it was the Indian pattern. Roughly speaking, one third of the finances for operating schools came from each of these sources: government grants-in-aid, fees from students, and appropriations from the mission board. Such government aid has not been an unmixed blessing. The schools are subject to government inspection. Generally this has been friendly, but often it has made for more rigid procedures, hampering experimentation and creativity.

So popular has been education that mission schools have been more often than not congested. The majority of students have ordinarily been non-Christians. On an India-wide basis these figures would not be far off for the percentage of Christians at various levels: primary schools, 50 per cent Christians; high school, 20 per cent; colleges, 6 per cent. Providing training for non-Christians has repeatedly been hotly debated. At one time the American Congregationalists and English Baptists closed their schools, but later they established others. Without them not only did they lack facilities for training Christian students, but they gained the ill-will of the community.

There have been three fundamental reasons for Christian schools in India:

1. To provide training at various levels for Christians. It is fearful to contemplate what might be the state of the church today, so largely of lowly origin, if schools had not been established.

2. To provide access to the minds of non-Christian students. Here the influence, both direct and indirect, has been incalculably great.

3. To serve and bear witness before the wider community and often to pioneer and set the standard for schools instituted under other auspices.

In recent years Christian schools in India have not been effective agencies for direct evangelism. Very often, though, they have "prepared the soil," as it were. Moreover they have proved effective to the onlooker who received no direct benefit but for whom the school stood as a public witness and reminder of what was being done in the name of Jesus. Many inquirers have cited this factor as first arousing their interest in the Christian faith.

Colleges

The Methodist Church is primarily responsible for two colleges, both located in Lucknow. We co-operate also in two in

Pakistan, Forman Christian College and Kinnaird College for Women, both in Lahore. The former especially has had a long and distinguished record. Its motto is a witness which Pakistan needs: "By Love Serve One Another." In India we co-operate in some degree also with other denominations in colleges at Nagpur, Bombay, and Madras.

Isabella Thoburn College, one of the really outstanding institutions of the country, was established in 1886. The Presbyterians also co-operate in it. Its enrollment is about 400, with students coming from all over the land, as well as from several foreign nations, and from all the major religious communities. Three fourths of the teaching staff are Christians. Training is given for both the B.A. and B.S. degrees as well as for the teachers' diploma. Instruction has always been of a high order, with constant emphasis on Christian development. In recent years especially considerable attention has been given to social service by the students. We can rightfully be proud of this splendid college.

Across the city is Lucknow Christian College with an enrollment of 800 men. Established in 1888, the college has rendered notable service through the years. Hindustani shorthand was devised there, and for years it had a strong commercial department. Today it grants both B.A. and B.S. degrees and has a teacher-training department. Its science courses have been strong; its physical education instruction ranks high throughout the subcontinent. Dr. C. M. Thacore is the capable Indian principal. The fine new Chitambar Memorial Chapel at the heart of the campus, largely the gift of Ohio Methodists, is a symbol of the Christian nature of the college and an increasingly useful means of uplifting the lives of its students.

High Schools

Out of the numbers of Methodist high schools, only two are selected for brief mention. One is Raewind Christian Institute near Lahore. It is the largest school for boys under Methodist auspices in Pakistan. As such it is of great importance for the development of a strong church in that land. There are 360 students ranging from primary grades to high school. Of these 160 are Christians. Also a part of the institute is a teacher-training department which has 130 students, the only such school for men under Christian auspices in West Pakistan. The headmaster, A. R. Samuel, was a Crusade Scholar. He is ably assisted by Mrs. Daisy Samuel. The institute has always emphasized the practical and has aimed at an all-round philosophy of Christian education. Recently it has been strengthened through Presbyterian co-operation and by new buildings furnished as a special gift from the Genesee Conference. The program of this school contributes to the solution of the two most acute problems of the church in Pakistan: need of trained leaders and improvement of economic life.

The story of this school's beginning is a part of the romance of missions. Nearly half a century ago the workers at Lahore were praying earnestly for a school to care for the growing number of Christians. One hot summer day a widow, a complete stranger, called and offered the money for such an institution as a memorial to her husband. Built first in Lahore, it was later moved to the Raewind site.

Away to the south in Hyderabad is the Stanley Girls' School. Its physical equipment is of the finest. Under the leadership of its present principal, Miss Chanda Christdas, herself an alumna, it has become one of the finest schools of its kind in India. Started with two students in 1895, the school is today crowded with 1,700 students, half of them Christians. Its home science department is one of the best in the country, yet thoroughly Indian in its approach. There is a seriousness and earnestness about Stanley. For years the girls have done social service in the community as an extracurricular activity. But it's not all intensity; for the atmosphere of Christian love is evident; they are happy students. The kindergarten associated with the school has 300 tots. It has the delightful name, Prem

Bagh—"The Garden Where Love Is." Among Stanley's graduates are many outstanding girls. One is Miss Edith DeLima, now principal of Baldwin Girls' School in Bangalore. Of another, while studying in the United States, a hostess testified: "I never expect to see her equal on earth."

In connection with most of the schools are hostels, or dormitories, where the students, usually only Christians from rural areas, are resident. In recent years the Christian opportunity in the dormitories has been recognized more fully and provided for. In the out-of-class hours the atmosphere of a Christian home-away-from-home affords opportunity to teach lasting habits of cleanliness, discipline, fair play, group living, study, and devotion.

Council of Christian Education

The youth work is closely related to Methodist schools. The Youth Department is an important part of the Council of Christian Education. The Council is under the capable direction of the Rev. Gabriel Sundaram. In recent years work among youth has increased by leaps and bounds. For example, during the Christmas holidays of 1953-54 thirteen young Indian Methodists and an equal number of I-3's, short-term missionaries, gathered together for a work camp near Delhi. They spent a week helping the villagers build their own church. For years the people in this village had wanted a church, but this group gave them the stimulus which resulted in their completing it themselves. This was for them all a great spiritual adventure. It was a demonstration of the dignity of labor and gave the villagers a sense of "belonging" to a world-wide Christian fellowship.

Another important activity of the youth movement is the sponsoring of gospel teams along the pilgrim routes of India. Such a route runs from the plains of northern India to a shrine of a Hindu deity at Badrinath, high in the snowy Himalayas. Each year thousands of pilgrims make their weary way along this road. Sometimes they suffer in the extreme. For several summers now Methodist young people have stationed themselves along this route to be of help to the pilgrims and to witness to them. For those who have participated it has been an unforgettable spiritual experience.

RURAL MINISTRY

Most Christians of Southern Asia live in rural India and Pakistan. Most of the institutions, however, are in urban centers and towns. Sometimes schools are criticized because they encourage young people to leave the villages for training and but few return. Answer: take the training and skills to the people where they live, by the use of extension methods.

Success with such methods did not come easily in the United States. One recalls the Virginia farmer years ago who said of the county agent: "What can this young fellow teach me about farming? Why I've worn out three farms!" Indian villagers are conservative too, but they are showing a new alertness; they are eager for something better. How often missionaries have felt heartache and frustration knowing that a *desire* for a higher standard has been aroused, but the means of attaining it are often absent! Let us observe some experiments toward such attainment.

Village Centers

A comprehensive approach to an adequate rural ministry is the village center. One type has developed during the last twenty-five years in the Hyderabad Conference under a missionary, the Rev. John Patterson, and an Indian colleague, the Rev. D. Gabriel. Christian centers are located in small market towns, natural centers for several villages round about. A small building partly open on one side is constructed to serve as a combination school and church. Flanking it on both sides are often two houses, one for the pastor and one for a teacher. The three buildings make a U-shape, forming a courtyard toward which the open side of the school-church is faced. If a large group assembles, the worship can overflow into the courtyard. Sometimes a one-room dispensary is added. Not infrequently the wife of the pastor or teacher is a nurse or midwife who can operate the dispensary.

Into these buildings are built chimneys and windows, neither of which most village houses have. Soon these are copied in other homes, so that windows and chimneys preach the gospel too. The center is provided with a bored-hole latrine, another innovation. The leaders are encouraged to keep poultry and raise a garden. Bishop J. W. Pickett, who twenty-five years ago surveyed the district where these centers have been planted, said it was then one of the worst rural church areas in the country but that now it is one of the best.

A similar approach is that set in operation by Miss Helen Fehr, a gifted missionary under the Woman's Division of Christian Service, in the Madhya Pradesh Conference. This center is located in a village where Miss Fehr herself often lives for periods in a mud and grass house costing about $50. With her Indian coworkers she uses demonstration methods in growing crops, raising improved poultry, keeping bees, goats, and cattle. Another feature is a "moving school," a bullock cart taking the demonstration methods to the people—improved seeds, literacy charts, public health information together with aids to worship. An effort is made to utilize materials readily available in rural India and methods which may easily be copied. It is intensely practical, studiedly simple. Another part of the program is the holding of short-term institutes for the training of women and laymen. Here again living standards have been raised visibly.

Christian Villages in a Muslim Land

Like Moses and the children of Israel, thirty years ago a missionary led a group of landless Christian followers to their promised land. A new irrigation scheme in the Punjab had

brought thousands of acres into cultivation. Through the efforts
of missionaries a tract was secured for Christians. Today
several entirely Christian villages exist there, in the Muslim
land of Pakistan. One of the villages is named after the "Moses"
of the venture—Stuntzabad, after Dr. Clyde B. Stuntz, long a
missionary in the Punjab.

Stuntzabad, now with a population of one thousand, stands
in marked contrast to typical villages in the subcontinent. The
streets are wide; the houses set apart from one another. A
retired preacher living there received a prize for having the neat-
est and cleanest house and yard in any village in the area.
Stuntzabad boasts a school up to the eighth grade, a church,
and a clinic operated by a Pakistani nurse. A missionary for
rural work is soon to be available to Stuntzabad and surrounding villages. He is trained in irrigation problems, so vital
in West Pakistan, of which the Psalmist might have written
(Psalm 63): "My soul thirsteth for thee . . . in a dry and
thirsty land."

This project becomes more significant in the light of a bit
of history. In 1902 it was decided to close the work in that
part of India as a sterile field of only 600 Christians. It was
not closed, however, and a few years later there were 70,000
Christians, half now in the Indus River Conference of Pakistan
and half in the Delhi Conference.

A Rural School

The Methodist Rural Middle School at Zaheerabad is excep-
tional, being right out in the country. A few years ago it was
wasteland. Now under the eyes and hands of George and
Elsie Garden and their colaborers it is blooming like a rose.

The school is really like a village, with some improvements
which ought to be and can be incorporated into villages themselves. The 150 boys and 60 girls live in small cottages—class-
rooms by day and sleeping rooms by night. They have neither

desks nor beds. Small mats on the floor serve for the former and long mats with blankets for the latter. That is according to village custom in the region.

The boys and girls do manual work for two and a half hours a day. That is revolutionary in India, where education is regarded as the way to escape working with one's hands. It is like Gandhi's Basic Schools, where one learns by doing, and the learning situation arises out of the events of everyday experience. One boy said recently, "Boy! I'm having fun here. I learn something new every day!" They take time off to help fight cholera in a near-by village. Because problems of the village are dealt with, children return to their village equipped to meet its demands.

Zaheerabad witnesses by deed and word. Each Saturday the boys go to some near-by village to put in practice what they learn. On one occasion as the boys entered a village, the people asked, "What are you doing?"

The boys and their teacher replied: "We have come to help you clean up some of these dirty drains. Flies and mosquitoes breed in these drains, and then you get typhoid and malaria and die."

"Is the government sending you here? Are they paying you for this?"

"No one sent us. We came because we are Christians. Our God teaches us to care about what happens to all the people everywhere. So we want to show you how you can drive malaria out of your village."

"This is very strange," the villagers said. "Please tell us more about your God and why you have come."

That night a large group of all sections of the village came to hear the boys give their testimonies telling of God's love for all men everywhere no matter what their caste or creed.

"Please come again," said the people as the boys started home in the moonlight.

Ingraham Institute

At Ingraham Institute near Delhi still another approach is used. In addition to a rural school, teachers are trained, manual arts are emphasized, and a well rounded program of rural extension is being developed. A young missionary, Henry A. Lacy, with a group of well qualified and inspired fellow workers, is bringing the training, equipment, and program to meet village needs.

Of special interest is village industry. Two types have thus far been inaugurated. One is the making of hasps and staples, the kind that used to be put on wooden chests and barn doors in this country. Using scrap steel and wire, dies are prepared and cut on a simple hand-operated press. The factory is provided rent-free by a village layman. It has a room on the roof which has become an "upper room"; there the workers start their day with worship. Sixteen man are producing 40 gross of hasps and staples a day and are entering into happy and productive lives.

Another venture is in the realm of leather. Many Christians in the region are traditional leatherworkers. The curing of hides is dirty, unpleasant work. Those who do it often sell the hides at an early stage in the process at prices too low to reward them for their labor. Ingraham has developed techniques by which the village can make a finished product of leather properly dyed and polished. Here again the gospel for *all* life is becoming a reality.

The significance of this venture is seen in the light of the fact that a million Christians in India are leather and hideworkers. And leather is a basic industry in any economy!

EVANGELISM

In a sense, it is a mistake to deal with evangelism as if it were a thing apart from other aspects of the Christian program. Rightly conceived, evangelism is inherent in every phase of work done in the name of Jesus Christ. The very act of service is a demonstration of the gospel. It is what someone has called "inevitable evangelism."

Following Independence, there was new interest on the part of educated Indians, and a number have been baptized. Evidently they had hesitated previously, fearing that to become a Christian would be to become less than Indian. The zeal of some of these new converts is amazing. One said: "I must share this news with India." Another told his Christian friends: "Raise your eyes and reckon all classes of Indians as in need of the gospel . . . You will find scores ready to accept as soon as you present Him." A third: "I tried Hinduism and Communism and was disappointed, but Christianity satisfied my mind and my heart. Millions in India can be won to Christ, and will be, if we who know Him present Him as He is." A leader has said that a Christian is not simply a person who worships Christ, for that is done by many Hindus; but that a Christian is one who *proclaims* Him.

A recent book on evangelism in India mentions some twenty methods. A few of the ways are: by posters, by newspapers, by visitation, by drama, by pictures, by song. One village preacher speaks of "friendship evangelism." Only three ways will be touched upon below.

The Jathra or Mela: Evangelism through Social Heritage

The *jathra* or *mela* is common in India. It is a kind of religious fair. Christian *melas* have developed in many parts of the country in recent years, an example of adapting the social heritage to serve the church. It is something like an old-fashioned camp meeting. Anywhere from a few hundred to several thousand people may attend. Sometimes special trains are operated to the sites. *Melas* are attractive not only because they are not foreign to the Indian culture; for there is movement, color, group participation, music. A social need is met; an effort is demanded of the individual, who sometimes walks miles to attend.

A famous Methodist center of this type is at Dharur between the South India and Hyderabad Conferences. The whole tone of the church round about has been improved by these camp meetings. For many villagers it has been the gateway to victorious living.

The Ashram: Evangelism through Fellowship

An *ashram* is a spiritual retreat, long used in Hinduism. In recent years a number of Christian ashrams have been instituted. One established by Dr. E. Stanley Jones at Sat Tal ("Seven Lakes") is located in the foothills of the Himalayas. Each May and June it is open, offering for many not only a change from the heat of the parched plains, but spiritual refreshment as well.

The ashram is an experiment in group living, affording for its participants an experience in disciplined fellowship. A framework of Christian devotion is set for the day. Within that framework provision is made for study and discussion, for manual work, for rest and recreation. The whole centers around Christ and an effort is made to live as if the ashram were a cell of the Kingdom. Folk of different backgrounds of nationality, race, religon, classes and professions unite as one family and ignore their barriers.

More important, the inner barriers of life—anxieties, fears, hatreds, frustrations—are exposed to the penetrating light of the Gospel. Many are untangled and then related in a renewing fellowship with Christ.

Mottoes hanging on the ashram wall are suggestive of the nature of the place: "Seek the truth, come whence it may, cost what it will."

"Here we enter a fellowship: sometimes we will agree to differ; always we will resolve to Love and unite to Serve."

"Let not this group *seek* the answer but *be* the answer."

"Philosophers have explained the world; we must now change it."

Leaflets: Evangelism through the Written Word

A new departure in India is called leaflet evangelism. Dr. John H. Piet of the Church of South India is largely responsible for its development. He came to the end of his first term as a missionary with the comfortable feeling that he had done a good job as a teacher in a college, but the uncomfortable feeling that he had won not one person to allegiance to Jesus Christ. He determined during his next term to do something about it. He had accepted it as a fact that every Christian is an evangelist. He therefore approached one of his Indian colleagues and asked why he did not evangelize. The colleague said that he was layman and that evangelism was the task of ministers. Thereupon Dr. Piet pointed out that every Christian is an evangelist and then asked his colleague if he would engage in active evangelism if he (Dr. Piet) would. The layman agreed.

There remained the decision as to method. They determined on "leaflet evangelism." During the first year of the second term a one-page pamphlet was taken every two months to each home in a large district. The subjects of these leaflets were "Meet Jesus Christ," "Read the Bible," "Come to Church," "Merry Christmas!" "Christian Social Work," "Easter." A second series was on Old Testament themes. Ten million leaflets have been distributed in a number of languages during the last five years.

The response has been great, and in a hitherto sterile district of South India a considerable interest has been aroused in Christianity. The leaflets were brought to focus also on the study of the Bible. At the present time in Dr. Piet's area thirteen thousand folk are engaged in correspondence Bible study.

Evangelism, the sharing of the good news of Christ, is the continuing task of the church. The church in Southern Asia urgently needs a new and widespread seriousness about this. There are islands of earnestness here and there. But there is danger that the church may solidify and consolidate its position rather than launch out on evangelism. The mission has produced a church; now the church must embark on its own mission.

One cannot but think of the figure of the Indian fisherman. All over the country he is to be seen. He drapes a circular net in a special way. Then, swinging it around his head, he casts it out over the water. It falls almost like a parachute in a perfect circle over the water, enclosing all within its grasp as its weighted edges sink beneath the surface. Then by a rope attached to the center, he draws it in. Cannot Christians in Pakistan and India do likewise?

A Methodist missionary is writing a book called, "The Hamlet of God." Upon being asked if his title was a parody of St. Augustine's "City of God," he stated that "hamlet" in Old English referred to a village in which there is no church. The evangelistic challenge is clear and urgent. There are tens of thousands of "hamlets" in India and Pakistan, and our task is not complete until they all become a part of the City of God!

We Labor Together

During recent years the Methodist record for co-operation in Southern Asia has been good. There is hardly a united Christian effort of any kind within the territory of its responsibility in which it is not bearing its full share. It was not always so. We have already seen that while William Butler preferred concentration in North India, Taylor and Thoburn were expansionists. The latter thought not of a mission *in* India but *for* India. This was often understood by others as disregard of comity, the mutual recognition of territorial responsibility by co-operating churches. Taylor's view did not sit well with other denominational leaders.

Gradually denominational rivalry gave way to co-operation and friendly consultation. Beginning in 1862 large interdenominational missionary conferences were held in various cities of India every ten years. Incentives from within and pressures from without joined to hasten the co-operative process. The foolishness of rivalry when many areas were unoccupied, the scandal of it before the non-Christian public, the unnecessary expense of duplication have all encouraged closer working together.

In many respects, co-operation and union have gone ahead further in mission fields than in the homelands. Union theological seminaries, apparently the last realm in which co-operative effort would be considered, are quite common in many mission lands, including Pakistan and India. Whether it be in education, medicine, literature production or the training of ministers, ways are found of working unitedly. The churches are discovering the simple truth that as long as they are walking the same road, they may walk together.

The National Christian Council of India

The National Christian Council of India was inaugurated in 1923. Prior to that time there was a National Missionary Council. The present organization is made up of not less than half Indians.

This organization has its headquarters in Nagpur, which is about the center of India. At the time of writing Bishop Shot K. Mondol of the Hyderabad Area is president of the National Christian Council. Bishop J. Waskon Pickett was formerly its presiding officer and Dr. Murray T. Titus a secretary. Bishop C. D. Rockey has from time to time sat with the Council. Three Methodist missionaries are now related to the organization: Dr. R. W. Scott, a secretary on the headquarters staff; Dr. Donald F. Ebright, secretary of the Audio-Visual Aids Committee; the Rev. Donald E. Rugh, director of the Relief Committee.

The Rev. William Paton, first secretary of the N.C.C., as the organization is usually called, issued a famous memorandum urging the churches to "act as if they were one." The council is co-ordinative and consultative rather than supervisory or functional in nature. It provides a channel for united effort.

The Relief Committee

One of these efforts finds expression in the Relief Committee. Both funds and contributions in kind are channeled by the Methodist Committee for Overseas Relief through Church World Service to this committee.

Soon after Independence in 1947 the Christian church was confronted with human need of truly Himalayan proportions. The largest mass migration in human history took place as millions of Muslims fled from India to Pakistan and millions of Sikhs and Hindus hastened from Pakistan to India. In addition to the thousands who were slaughtered, more thousands were sick and wounded.

The church acted promptly and unitedly. Dr. E. C. Bhatty, a secretary of the N.C.C. rushed to the scene. The situation was such between the Hindus and Muslims that each group was reluctant and fearful to accept aid from the other. Both trusted the Christians. Dr. Bhatty said: "Truly man's calamity proved to be God's opportunity. In no other situation could this be so literally true as it was in this case. God had opened the gates wide for the church to enter into compassionate service. This indeed was a clear call and a unique challenge for the Church in India and abroad . . ."

A summons was sent out for volunteer aides of every type, particularly doctors and nurses. Teams assembled from all parts of the subcontinent and helped in the refugee camps. One of these was at a place called Kurukshetra, a famous battlefield of Hindu lore. There during the last days of his life Mahatma Gandhi for a whole morning watched a Methodist surgeon operate on wounded refugee patients. Among the last scenes on which the aged Mahatma's tired eyes rested were the deeds of love and mercy performed where centuries ago there had been bloodshed. One Hindu observing the sight said: "I have seen today a re-enactment of the Parable of the Good Samaritan." Christians on the Pakistan side of the border were performing similar works. Thus early in the national life of these two countries Christians could establish their neutrality and exercise a ministry of reconciliation. Of Christians the first Indian Governor-General, C. Rajagopalachari, could say with respect to this aid: "They are the most patriotic citizens of the country."

Similar relief activity has continued with clothing and blankets, tons of powdered milk, millions of vitamin tablets, and food concentrates being distributed wherever need arose. An effort has been made to make these supplies available where needed without respect to creed.

Audio-Visual Aids Committee

In India today as in Palestine of old people say, "We would see Jesus." The Audio-Visual Aids Committee holds training institutes, publishes a periodical, maintains film libraries, makes recordings of music and gospel messages for broadcast, prepares film.

One of the important contributions of this committee is to put into the hands of a village preacher other means than simply the human voice to convey his message. An alert preacher can readily obtain training in the use of flannel-graph materials, of cartoon "jets," in projection of slides and film strips from a machine lighted by a kerosene lantern.

Dr. James E. McEldowney of Leonard Theological College has organized a splendid audio-visual department there in relationship with this committee. He has been responsible for the production of three sound films in the Indian setting: "The Prodigal Son," "The Good Samaritan," and "The Story of the Transformed Life," about Zacchaeus. These films are proving very effective. In Bombay following the showing of one of them, under apparently very poor circumstances, two Hindus became inquirers. A lady present said: "I've been a professing Christian for years, but never before today did I sense the presence of God in my life."

The Board of Christian Literature

Christian literature has always been a main interest of the church in mission lands. This was clearly true in the earliest days in which there were Bible translations, publications on Indian religion and culture, Christian apologetic literature to be used in evangelism, books for the use of Christians. Then came a period in which both quality and quantity of Christian books diminished, for literature was too often lost sight of in the midst of a great variety of activity.

Happily, during the years since Independence interest has revived in this important matter. A battle for the minds of men is going on in India today. The forces which can produce and distribute the most challenging literature will carry the most influence in the generation ahead. In such a crucial situation, once again, more can be accomplished by united action than otherwise. What are some of the things which are being fostered by the N.C.C. in the field of literature?

First of all, inspired by Dr. Frank Laubach, a School of Journalism was established in 1952 at Hislop College in Nagpur; for qualified writers were needed. The first year forty-two students completed the course. A number of these are now engaged in Christian literature production. One edits a newsletter for the Allahabad Agricultural Institute.

Another undertaking with which the N.C.C. is related is called World Christian Books. It is aimed at meeting the need for simple, moderately priced books on Christian themes for the average educated layman. Thirty books in all are planned, some to be written by younger churchmen. They will be prepared for translation and adaptation to various languages. Bishop Stephen Neill is the general editor and comes to his task from a rich background. The first titles are: *The Christians' God, Christian Giving, Studying the Bible Today, Religion and Science*. With the coming of these books the village preacher, too, may finally have a small library in addition to his Bible and hymnbook—too often his only literary tools for a difficult and complicated task!

Moreover the committee is providing for special literature for educated youth and for the intelligentsia, groups of special importance. The former are asking the usual questions on religion and nationalism; education and life; sex, marriage and the home; international affairs. Books and pamphlets are being prepared on such subjects.

All of this requires good printing presses. One of the best is the recently built and newly equipped Lucknow Publishing House of the Methodist Church under the Rev. W. W. Bell.

Of related if not prior importance is the training of people to read. Under a variety of auspices this is going on all over India. What Dr. Frank Laubach and his associates have done to stimulate this is well known. Often school children devote some of their holiday periods to teaching the illiterate to read.

There is greater need than ever for the church in India and Pakistan to feel the challenge of literacy. Christians are a people of the Book. To help open the gateway to Bible reading and a fuller knowledge of the living God is a magnificent challenge!

Some Union Institutions

Aside from taking part in consultative organizations, Methodists co-operate with other denominations in Pakistan and India in no less than forty union institutions of various types. Let us look at a few.

United Christian Hospital, Lahore

Established in 1947, this hospital is a "child of Partition" and the refugee situation which accompanied it. Just as on the India side of the border Christians stepped into the breach at the time, so in Lahore. The hospital is situated on the campus of the Forman Christian College, occupying two former dormitory blocks. In this institution Methodists work together with Presbyterians, United Presbyterians, and Anglicans. This is

now one of the best hospitals in the country. It has 175 beds.
A recent grant from the Methodist Committee for Overseas
Relief has supplied a tuberculosis mobile unit. In the Nurses'
Training School are many Muslim girls, who until recently
have been reluctant to undertake nursing as it was not considered respectable work. Thus Christians can maintain a lead
in this field in Pakistan as in India and greatly serve their
country. The Methodist Church has two missionary doctors
on the staff, both formerly having served in China, and a public health nurse.

Another doctor at the United Christian Hospital is a plastic
surgeon. This, too, is an important field for Christian witness.
Not only is he able to remove blemishes which mar his patients
outwardly, but he also testifies to One who can transform them
within.

Two or three years ago there was held in Karachi the organizing session of the All-Pakistan Medical Association. Other
nations were invited to send doctors. The Soviet Union sent
four doctors on a chartered plane. Belatedly the United States
Embassy asked two American medical missionaries from this
hospital to attend. One of them was the plastic surgeon. At
first the Russian doctors evoked great interest as they told of
the accomplishments of the healing art in their homeland. This
was about the time when Russia was claiming most of the
principal medical discoveries of modern times. The Pakistani
doctors were all ears.

The time came for the plastic surgeon to tell of his work,
which he illustrated by "before and after" slides in color. Then
the Pakistani doctors gathered around the two American missionaries. They were asked: "We know where the Russian
doctors came from. They were flown down from Moscow. But
where did you come from?" The reply was, "We didn't come
from anywhere. We were already here!" Typical missionaries
are already there, not as propaganda experts, not as apologists
for the American way of life, but there to serve in every possible

way and to witness to Jesus Christ as they may have opportunity.

Leonard Theological College, Jabalpur

Leonard Theological College was established in 1922. Originally it was solely a Methodist venture but since 1949 seven
other denominations have been co-operating in its program.
Training is through the medium of English and instruction leads
to the Bachelor of Divinity degree. Associated with the seminary
are a School of Religious Education, a Women's School, and a
Post-Graduate School. At present there are ninety-two students.
Since Leonard enjoys a central location, students come from
nine different church backgrounds and from twelve different
language areas. The college is under the capable leadership of
Dr. Marvin H. Harper.

The seal and symbol of Leonard is a Syrian cross rising out
of a lotus. The lotus or water lily is of rich meaning in the Indian cultural heritage. It may be interpreted as representing
India's longing, her unfulfilled spiritual aspirations. The cross
—is the answer to that longing. Written on each side of the
cross are the words in Greek, "Living Way."

The refrain of the Leonard hymn is significant:

> "Show us Jesus!" Hear the cry of
> Multitudes in thronging mart!
> Send us, Lord, our Pentecost to
> Bear the Cross to India's heart.

An important new departure is the Department of Organized
Research. It is related to the Post-Graduate School and was
inaugurated by Dr. Henry H. Presler. It endeavors to train
students in scientific methods of research, related to the environ-
ment in which as Christians they are living. Some examples
of the problems they have studied are: the shift since Independence in English-speaking churches from Anglo-Indian to
largely Indian membership; a study of what happens to tradi-

tionally rural Christians who move to a city; the economic bases of a city congregation; studies of various Hindu sects. Such undertakings will serve an increasingly useful purpose in a developing church.

Leonard students engage in active field work of various kinds, including a Christian reading room in Jabalpur and the production of religious dramas. Indians are born actors. Professor C. Stanley Thoburn has written several Christian dramas, performed by the students.

Allahabad Agricultural Institute

Since 1945 Methodists have co-operated with seven other denominations in Allahabad Agricultural Institute, established by the Presbyterians. It is not only interdenominational in character, but international too. Its faculty is made up of forty-five well-trained Indians and ten missionaries; students number about 325. This group comes from lands as widely separated as New Zealand and the United States; Kenya and the Fiji Islands. It now has its first Indian principal, Oxford and Cornell trained, Henry S. Azariah, son of the famous Anglican, Bishop Azariah of Dornakal. The institute is widely recognized for its valued work in behalf of India. One agricultural expert from the West was called as a consultant by the Government of India on farm problems. Having surveyed the situation, he pointed to Allahabad and said: "That's the answer."

It was not always so. The founder, Dr. Sam Higginbottom, a Presbyterian missionary, encountered difficulties common to pioneers. As with other instances of "practical application" of the gospel, there were those who saw no place for the agricultural emphasis in the Christian program. How easily they had lost sight of the Parable of the Sower! Higginbottom wrote a book entitled *The Gospel and the Plow* in which he demonstrated his point. Some of the land he secured for the institute was wasteland. But he showed how to redeem it and so helped in one of India's deepest economic necessities—the recovery of fertility to the soil. What before 1911, the year of founding, was a dream is now a vivid reality in brick and mortar and men and women.

Today there is training at Allahabad in five different agricultural pursuits. It also offers splendid training in home economics. Students of all religious backgrounds come; they live and eat together—which means progress in India; they learn together and go out to serve together. Hardly a state in India and Pakistan today is without its Allahabad-trained agricultural supervisors.

The Institute is not just academic. Its fine extension department, financed by the Ford Foundation, constitutes one of the fifty-five Community Projects under the Five Year Plan. It reaches out a helping hand to 350 villages. The workers are called "village companions" who guide the people where they are ready to go in accord with an awakened sense of need. Their motto is: "Companionship, not force."

Another development is a factory for manufacturing farm implements—adapted to Indian conditions. How many missionaries have thought to revolutionize Indian agriculture by ordering an old horse-drawn soil-turning plow from Sears and Roebuck, only to discover that the bullocks or oxen, the only animal power available to the villager, could not pull the plow! Allahabad has devised several soil-turning plows which bullocks can pull, thus replacing the unsatisfactory pointed-stick type of plow, like those shown in Ancient History books as used of old in Mesopotamia! One plow is called the "Wah-wah!" Hindi for "Oh boy!" which was what a farmer exclaimed when he first saw it in use. Another is called the *Shabash* plow, Hindustani for "well done." Some of the implements have been stamped out of the sheet steel coverings of armored cars used in World War II—literally swords beaten into plowshares!

The aim is to integrate the whole program as an expression of the Christian faith. The great theologian, Emil Brunner, was helpful by his lectures and presence at the Institute, for he had real insight into its problems. He jokingly said to the principal: "It's a good thing you invited me to talk about Christianity and the soil. So and so [naming a great European theologian] would not have understood it. Likewise [naming an American theologian] would have been insensitive to the subject. Another theologian could have helped you, but he's been dead four hundred years—Martin Luther!"

Vellore Christian Medical College

Vellore Christian Medical College is a great Christian institution. It probably represents the most extensive interdenominational co-operation of any service institution in the world, with forty Christian groups united in its work. The Minister of Health of India says of it, "Vellore is far ahead of any other medical college in India."

The founder of Vellore, Dr. Ida Scudder, came from a great family of missionaries, most of them medical people, who collectively have given over twelve hundred years of service in Asia. Ida Scudder was herself born in India in 1870. She had determined *not* to be a missionary. As a young woman, however, she was visiting her parents in India. During the course of one night, three men came for help for their wives in difficult childbirth. Her doctor father was not allowed, according to the then prevailing custom, to minister to conservative non-Christian women. So they were beyond available help. She determined then and there to train as a doctor and serve Indian women.

And what a missionary! In 1902 under the Arcot Mission of the Reformed Church of America she started a small hospital for women. In 1918 a medical school for women was opened. In 1947 it became a coeducational institute. Methodists have co-operated since 1945 and at this writing twenty-five students are Methodists. Dr. Ida, as she is called, has rendered a great Christian service to India.

Today Vellore has an outstanding hospital and school of nursing as well as the medical college. At the heart of both the hospital and the medical college premises, the latter about four miles away, are Christian chapels built on Indian architectural lines. This is appropriate for at heart Vellore is thoroughly and unashamedly a Christian institution. Its first Indian principal, Dr. Hilda Lazarus, was once about to operate. The patient suddenly objected that according to astrology, the time was not right for the operation. Dr. Lazarus replied, "We too work under a star, the Star of Bethlehem!" and proceeded with a successful operation.

The college extends its work out into the village with its famous roadside dispensaries. Vellore is interested in eyes, for there are estimated to be 500,000 operable cases of cataract in India. Many of them recover sight through the Mobile Eye Unit at eye camps.

Vellore is interested in hands. Dr. Paul Brand is a British orthopedic surgeon. At Vellore he became interested in leprosy. This disease damages hands in two ways. For one thing, the sense of touch is lost and unfelt injuries left untreated often cause loss of fingers, due to secondary infections. Furthermore a "claw-hand" develops, so that the fingers cannot be extended. Dr. Brand discovered that there is a strong grip in the closed "claw-hand." Moreover he found that leprosy did not affect the nerves which stimulate the muscles which closed the hands. Then he used his skill as an orthopedic surgeon to reconnect tendons to good muscles so that, in a word, the hand could be opened as well as closed. It is almost as if the voice of Jesus is heard again through the centuries: "Stretch forth thy hand."

Vellore is interested in hearts. Methodists should be proud of their representatives in Vellore, Dr. and Mrs. Reeve Betts. Originally Baptists, they are supported on the field by Methodist churches in Richmond and Ann Arbor. Dr. Betts is one of the world's leading chest surgeons. Instead of using his skill for a lucrative practice at home, he devotes himself to

Christ and to India's people. His thoracic unit and training of chest surgeons is outstanding.

Ludhiana Christian Medical College

Away to the north of India is Ludhiana, where in 1894 with four students Dr. Edith Brown started a medical college for women, the first of its kind in all Asia. An English Baptist, she later received the feminine counterpart of a "knighthood" and was known as *Dame* Edith Brown. In 1952 this school too became coeducational, and during the same year Methodists united with other boards in service there. Our representatives are Dr. Margaret Tucker, a radiologist, and an orthopedic surgeon, Dr. Ronald Garst.

Talk of humble beginnings! The first dissecting room had been a latrine. But Dame Brown was, if anything, determined. More than 600 women doctors have gone forth from Ludhiana; and in 1953 two thousand applied though only fifty new students could be admitted. They will be joined by many others, men and women; for in March 1954, the Health Minister of India, Raj Kumari ("Princess") Amrit Kaur dedicated a new modern five-hundred-bed hospital. This was a venture of faith, for money for only one fourth of its cost was in hand. Raj Kumari quoted Gandhiji regarding this (she was once his secretary): "No good work ever languishes from lack of funds. It languishes for lack of good workers." The principal, Dr. Eileen Snow, could reply, "We are trying to educate doctors who care more for patients than for money . . . we are trusting in God who has led us thus far to provide the rest."

Related to Ludhiana are a nurses' training school, a tuberculosis hospital, a leprosarium, and an active new public health department. India has only one doctor to each seven thousand people and one nurse to each forty-five thousand. Numbers alone indicate a need for Ludhiana for a long time to come. As for those devoted to selfless service, what country has enough of such folk?

CHURCH UNION

Representatives of the various denominations have discovered their oneness in action. Theirs is a common task in common obedience to One Lord. Dr. John Mackay calls this the "unity of the road." As the prophet Amos said: "Shall two walk together, except they have agreed?" The reunion of the churches has for decades been a live issue in India.

The tragedy of disunity is costly. A number of years ago the Ezhava caste of Hindus in South India, representing nearly a million people, desired to enter the Christian church. There arose the disconcerting question, "Which church will you join?" They had supposed Christians were one people. Having had experience of disunity in Hinduism, they desired no more of that. So they lost interest. That bit of history has a footnote. In a report written in January 1953, this phrase occurs: "It is worth noting also that the greatest number of Travancore Communists come from the Ezhava community . . ."

Much has been accomplished toward unity. On September 27, 1947, only a little over a month after Indian Independence, the Church of South India was inaugurated. The year 1947 will be as much a landmark for the church as it is for the Indian nation. That year saw the most comprehensive union in church history, with Christians of five different traditions becoming one: Anglicans, Methodists (British), Reformed, Presbyterian, Congregationalists. Some have called it "the most significant event in ecclesiastical history since the Reformation." It is interesting that this first union of churches of episcopal and non-episcopal types should have taken place in a mission land.

This union did not come about easily. For twenty-eight years the parties negotiated, each trying to preserve his own tradition. Finally, they ceased this selfish effort. Real progress came when all came to the place of seeing that the real incentive for union was that it was the will of God. When they all could say: "Thy will be done!" union was possible.

The Methodist Church in Southern Asia, except for a brief period of consultation, never actively negotiated for participation in the Church of South India. It has, however, negotiated in a similar plan for North India.

The North India plan is called the Round Table scheme. It represents consultation of a group of churches since 1929. At present it involves the following groups in both India and Pakistan: Anglicans, British Baptists, British Methodists, the United Church of North India (including former Presbyterians and Congregationalists) and American Methodists. In repeated meetings of representatives of these bodies a Basis of Union and a proposed constitution have been hammered out. These are being referred to the governing bodies of the several churches involved. The necessary steps *could* be taken so that union is *possible* by 1959. In the case of Methodists the plan must be studied by Annual Conferences, the General Conference of 1956, and the Central Conference following that.

The barriers to agreement have not been form of government nor doctrinal position. The real problems are (1) mutual recognition of the ministries of the various churches, and (2) the unification of two types of episcopacy, Anglican and Methodist.

The former problem confronted the Church of South India. They met it by proclaiming a thirty-year period during which mutual recognition would be given to various ministers. After that the church of a later generation would have to decide. In the Round Table plan the ministry will be unified from the beginning through a mutual "laying-on of hands of the duly authorized persons of the other churches" thus accepting "additional authority they lack in separation." This "is not reordination; nor is it presumed to bestow again the grace, gifts, character, or authority that have already been bestowed on them."

Regarding the two types of bishops, a similar mutual recognition will be arranged. Thus the Anglicans will share the "historic" episcopate "which is in historic continuity with that of the early Church. No particular theological interpretation of episcopacy, as accepted in the United Church, is thereby implied or shall be demanded from any minister or member thereof." In other words, it does not mean acceptance of "apostolic succession." On the other hand, the "spiritual heritage" of the Methodist episcopacy as a method of church government would be shared by the new church.

One cannot predict what may develop. Though fears of various kinds are voiced, the prevailing mood among Christians in India is for union. Along that road great power and effectiveness are possible. God makes His will clear to those who are ready to obey.

Into Nepal

The outer borders of the Indo-Pakistan subcontinent are rimmed about by "closed lands:" closed to the gospel and to many other outside influences. Saudi Arabia, Afghanistan, Tibet, Nepal, Sikkim, and Bhutan—these are the closed lands. Recently one of them, Nepal, opened a little for work of the Christian church. It had been closed since 1771 when the few Roman Catholic missionaries there were directed to leave.

How did the door open? There was a lot of prayer, continued for years by those who deeply longed to witness to Nepal. Dr. Robert Fleming was a lay missionary teaching at Woodstock School in the Himalayas. He was asked by Chicago's Field Museum to go into Nepal to collect bird specimens. This he did during three winter vacations beginning in 1940-50. On one expedition he was accompanied by his wife, Dr. Bethel Fleming, a physician; on another by Dr. Carl Friedericks, a Presbyterian medical missionary. They made friends with Nepalese officials; and when in February 1953 they wrote asking permission to open medical work at two places in the little country, it was granted.

Meanwhile, in the summer of 1952, a group of dedicated technical experts started Point IV work in Nepal. At the capital city, Kathmandu, they held their own church services and Sunday school each week. This was in marked contrast to the custom of many Americans overseas. This group showed how religion is practiced on "Main Street" back home. Undoubtedly they helped to dispose the minds of Nepalese officials favorably to the missionaries.

Nepal is mountainous. The southern slopes of Everest lie within her borders. Annapurna is there and a score of other very high peaks. In size and shape it is about equivalent to Tennessee; it lies a "buffer state" between India and Tibet. For over a hundred years it was ruled by the strong hands of hereditary prime ministers until 1951, when a revolution restored the king to active rule through democratic processes. It is now an independent kingdom.

Nepal is the home of some ten million people. Only two per cent are literate; only one per cent have had access to anything like modern medicine. The popular religion is a mingling of Hinduism and Buddhism. Nepal's only real export has been soldiers. The Gurkha is one of the world's best fighters. Each year some of them join the Indian and British armies. Though cut off from much of the outside world, the Nepalese are cheerful, strong, and possessed of some remarkable qualities.

On January 7, 1954, the first of five maternity and child welfare centers was started in the Valley of Kathmandu, the capital. A few months before two British women doctors started medical work at Pokhara to the northwest. A few months later Dr. Friedericks began a small hospital at Tansen, a hundred miles west of the capital. Two Mar Thoma Christians hold services for a few Christians who have made their way to Kathmandu. Now the people throng the doors of the dispensaries to receive treatment. Hundreds of people in the medical centers are for the first time feeling the touch of the Great Physician.

Meanwhile under the auspices of the N.C.C. of India a United Christian Mission to Nepal was organized. It is hoped that by co-operation through this body, *one* united Christian witness may be given. It is planned too that the missionary force shall be international in character, emphasizing not European missionaries, but Indians and Nepalese who in India have become Christians. This is a new pattern. It is not Methodist work in Nepal, but united *Christian* work.

The missionaries, when they first went to Kathmandu, were housed briefly in a palace. They had not lived in one before. Then they were told it was a "Class C" palace. So they had to swallow their pride. There are "Class A" palaces too in Kathmandu. Can one be for Christ the King?

In Conclusion

This little book began with a reference to John Wesley. It closes with a reference to him. In Lincoln College, Oxford, is a room restored to appear as it did when Wesley studied there. There the "Holy Club" met. In a corner today is a globe map of the world as it was in the 18th Century. How appropriate for the room of one who later conceived of the world as his parish!

We have visited a part of that parish, now enlarged to touch much of Pakistan and India. The year 1956 marks a hundred years of Indian Methodism. Soon our colleagues will head into a second century. What it holds, no one knows. Times and seasons are in the Father's hands. Perhaps it will afford much evidence of what the church in India and Pakistan can do for *us*. The task will have to be done in ever greater terms of fellowship and co-operation. It will have to be done in love, if the work is to be lasting. As He has raised up Butlers, Thoburns, Robinsons, Chitambars, Picketts, and so many more, surely He can raise up still others for His purposes.

Hear this parable! A Methodist missionary, Mary Reed, herself infected with the disease, had given her life to serve among those who were afflicted with leprosy and was stationed at Pithoragarh, remote in the Himalayas. Bishop Frank Warne prior to his retirement visited her for the last time. When he had departed a little down the path, he turned and Mary Reed shouted: "Hitherto!" [1] To which he replied: "Henceforth!"

---

[1] I Samuel 7:12.

INDEX